Parenting Plan Idea Workbook

Options for Child Custody Agreements and Time-Sharing

Lisa Wilson, CDC® | Gretchen Baskerville

Life Saving Press

PARENTING PLAN IDEA WORKBOOK: Options for Child Custody Agreements and Time-Sharing
by Lisa Wilson, CDC® and Gretchen Baskerville

Published by Life Saving Press LLC
30767 Gateway Pl., PMB 112
Rancho Mission Viejo, CA 92694

This material, including the coaching seminars mentioned in this book, is designed to provide information about the subject matter is covered. It is sold with the understanding that neither of the authors are giving legal, mental health, or other professional advice or services within the material. Every state is different, so if expert advice, legal services, or counseling are needed for your particular area, the reader should find and use the services of licensed professionals in their jurisdiction, for example an attorney licensed to practice in your state. The authors assume no responsibility for any damages incurred as a result of using this information.

For coaching and workshops on parenting plans, go online to: www.ParentingPlans101.com

Cover Image: ©2023 Canva Stock photo.

Print ISBN-13 (Paperback): 978-1-7343747-3-5
eBook ISBN-13: 978-1-7343747-4-2
BISAC code: LAW038010 **LAW** / Family Law / Children

Printed in the United States of America. First printing 2025

TABLE OF

Contents

DEDICATION

Lisa Wilson

To my children – your strength, resilience, and love have been my greatest inspiration. This work is dedicated to you, with hope that it helps create a gentler path for others walking a similar journey.

Gretchen Baskerville

For my children whose courage and laughter turned challenges into new beginnings – may your journeys always be filled with hope and faith.

INTRODUCTION

INTRODUCTION:
"What should I request in my parenting plan agreement?"

Good parents want a safe, peaceful, nurturing, and happy future for their children. The purpose of this *Parenting Plan Idea Workbook* is to aid in the parenting plan decision-making process while raising awareness of situations that may come up during and post-separation or divorce, helping you think through a variety of options that might work for your children, while keeping each parent's preferances in mind.

It is important to remember that you have a say in the decisions. This idea workbook will help you organize your thoughts so you can confidently discuss ideas with your attorney, mediator, or legal professional. Likewise, it is helpful to be knowledgeable and aware of common words and phrases to feel more comfortable during the parenting plan design process.

The end result, after working with an attorney, mediator or legally trained divorce professional, will be an official Parenting Plan Agreement which, if agreed to by both parties prior to the final divorce decree, will be a contractual agreement between the parents. This is typically created prior to a hearing or the court's official judgment, laying out what each parent is required to do in the future. In the event that an agreement is not reached prior to a hearing, your attorney or mediator can use the information gathered in this workbook to modify your parenting plan and help you negotiate with the other parent.

Given that you and the other parent may not always agree, it may be beneficial to have considered a Plan A (and ideal arrangement) and a Plan B (an acceptable compromise). Likewise, some requests may not conform to your state's guidelines, and/or may be rejected by the judge. As the statutes and regulations vary by state, your attorney or legal professional can give legal advice specific to your state and situation. They will also prepare the final legal documents suited to your state's guidelines for the court to approve. It is highly likely that the court will require the other parent's approval and agreement as well. With that in mind, it is important to work through the worksheet focused on options that your co-parent is likely to agree with in a settlement.

This workbook is divided into multiple sections to help you think through some parenting plan considerations.

- Describing your child(ren) and focusing on their needs
- Thinking through parenting plan ideas and evaluating these with your attorney
- Considering various custody or time-sharing calendars
- Determining your ideal plan and possible compromises

The overall intention of the workbook is to facilitate the parenting plan thought process as well as help you to be more prepared in the discussions with your attorney or legal professional when creating the formalized final parenting plan agreement.

USING A CO-PARENTING APP IS IMPORTANT

We strongly recommend that both parents invest in a co-parenting app for their smartphone or computer to document their discussions and note the time and date. These apps allow you to share parenting time calendars, checklists, and communication about important issues such as healthcare or schoolwork. They make it very difficult for a person to lie about sending, receiving, or reading emails or text messages. There are many apps available on the market at various prices. *See* ***Section 3-C: Communication and Information Sharing Considerations***, for some options, and do an internet search to find new options in various price ranges. Sometimes scholarships are available for those who are low income. Likewise, you may want to ask your attorney for a recommendation. Sometimes the judge will require both parents to use one.

PARENTING PLAN AGREEMENT TIPS

Introduction

The following questions and worksheets are designed to stimulate your thinking about how parenting may change as a result of the divorce. It's worth your time and energy to anticipate the challenges now and create a mutually agreeable parenting plan so that you both can work smoothly together in the future.

Key Considerations for Parenting Plans

1. **Children's Needs:**
   - Your child(ren) need stable routines, safety, love, and acceptance.
   - They also need a life free from tension and conflict. A well-crafted parenting plan now will help reduce distress later.

2. **Legal Guidelines:**
   - Your state and county have guidelines that govern child custody decisions.
   - Educate yourself by seeking the advice of a legal professional in your jurisdiction.

3. **Children's Input (Varies by Court):**
   - Some courts may allow your child(ren) to have a say in decisions surrounding time-sharing, while others do not.
   - Get advice from your attorney or legal professional on what is allowable in your area.

4. **Setting Boundaries:**
   - Good boundaries make good co-parents. It is important for both parents to know the rules.
   - Rules for one parent may also apply to both.

5. **Level of Detail in the Agreement:**
   - In some cases, detailed specifications in the agreement can be helpful.
   - In others, overly detailed or complex specifications may make life more difficult.
   - Your attorney can guide you in the best direction.

Using the Workbook

- This workbook is meant to help organize your thoughts before meeting with your attorney or mediator.
- **It is not recommended to share your written answers with the other parent or with a child custody evaluator without your attorney or legal professional's approval.**
- Taking time to go through the workbook can save stress and potentially reduce costs in the future.

Consulting Legal Professionals

Once you have thought through these points:

- Contact an attorney, mediator, or legal professional for state-specific legal advice.
- They will inform you about what is suitable for your situation.

Common Custody Arrangements

1. **Joint Physical Custody:**
    - Child(ren) live with and are cared for by both parents.
    - Parents often share physical custody about 50/50, unless there are circumstances such as criminal behavior, abuse, neglect, or other serious issues that make this arrangement unsuitable.

2. **Joint Legal Custody:**
    - Both parents have legal authority to make decisions regarding the child(ren).

    Note: Joint custody is common but may not always be the best arrangement. If this does not suit your child(ren), be prepared to explain why to your lawyer or a judge.

Benefits of an Agreed Parenting Plan

- The court-ordered divorce decree is often less detailed than an agreement designed by parents.
- Agreeing on a parenting plan outside of court provides more influence over the finalized document.

Importance of a Well-Crafted Plan

- The final parenting plan agreement should:
    - Serve the best interests of the child(ren).
    - Spell out solutions to common parenting issues.
    - Minimize conflict to protect the child(ren)'s health and wellbeing.

- Research shows that conflict, whether observed or sensed, is hard on children. Developing a thorough agreement upfront can safeguard their wellbeing, making this one of the most important documents created during a divorce.

1

GETTING STARTED

How to work with your attorney or mediator, the other parent, and the Court

GETTING STARTED – SECTION 1

As a starting point, this section is designed to help you list your greatest concerns and most preferable outcomes for a formalized Parenting Plan Agreement.

Children List the child(ren) below that are born to, adopted by, or dependents of the parties that the parenting plan agreement will cover.

Name Date of Birth

____

____

____

____

____

____

____

____

Your Hopes, Dreams, and Concerns for Your Child(ren)

As you embark on this journey of evaluating various considerations and possibilities for a parenting plan agreement for your separation or divorce, it is always a good idea to first determine your biggest concerns as well as your most preferable outcomes.

Describe below your three greatest hopes as well as concerns regarding your child(ren). While it is entirely possible that these may change as you go through the separation or divorce process, it can be beneficial to think through these questions in the beginning. Sometimes it can also help to revisit your answers to these questions as a tool for re-grounding yourself, if the process becomes overwhelming. You can use the answers as a reminder on your most important factors concerning your child(ren), helping you avoid getting "stuck in the weeds" during the process.

Biggest Hope/Concern #1

____

____

____

____

Biggest Hope/Concern #2

Biggest Hope/Concern #3

Describe below your most preferable outcomes regarding your child(ren) that you would like to see addressed in a finalized parenting plan agreement.

Preferable Outcome #1

Preferable Outcome #2

Preferable Outcome #3

2

DESCRIBING YOUR CHILD(REN)

Focus on what is best for each child.
One size doesn't fit all.

DESCRIBING EACH CHILD – SECTION 2

The following is a list of questions about your child(ren) to consider prior to filling out the Parenting Plan Worksheet. Do this exercise for each child being impacted by the divorce. While you contemplate the questions, notice particularities about your child(ren) that may influence how they might respond to the parenting agreement arrangements.

How would you describe this child? Name ________________________________

____

____

____

____

____

What makes this child special and unique?

____

____

____

____

Describe any special conditions (for example, school, medical, etc.) that are currently present. Any allergies, food sensitivities, etc.?

____

____

____

____

What are some challenges you have faced with your child in the past?

____

____

____

____

How has your child reacted to change in the past?

When dealing with change, what strategies have previously helped your child?

What activities and extra-curricular activities does your child currently participate in?

What activities and extra-curricular activities do you expect your child will participate in as they grow older? At what age do you expect your child to drive and have access to a car?

What are your child's hobbies?

How do you currently handle discipline with your child?

What kind of discipline does this child respond to best?

Have there been any changes in behavior in your child since becoming aware of the separation or divorce? If so, describe.

What do you think will be the most important concerns or challenges for your child, from their perspective, as they navigate life after the separation or divorce?

What do you think will be the least important issues for your child going forward after the separation or divorce?

What, if anything, do you think your child will like about life post-separation or divorce?

Which individuals are most integral and important in your child's life, and why?

Is there any adult, teenage friend and/or relative that your child should not have close contact with, and why?

What are each parents' current work schedules, overnight availability, and/or travel requirements? How will the child be supervised? And what changes are you expecting?

What information do you feel would be beneficial to share between households along with the time-sharing calendar? (for example, school/homework status, extracurricular activity updates, friendship concerns, health updates, behavioral discipline actions/progress, etc.)

What are the current mental health needs of the child? What are the anticipated future mental health or counseling/therapy needs of the child? Are they receiving therapy now? (If you wish to continue therapy in the future, it is best to start that therapy before the divorce is filed or before any hearings.)

Do you have any special concerns about <u>your</u> relationship with the other parent that needs to be addressed in the agreement? If so, please explain.

Do you have any special concerns about <u>your child's</u> relationship with the other parent that needs to be addressed in the agreement? If so, please explain.

What can you and the co-parent do to keep your child from observing or hearing conflict during and after the divorce?

Have there been any incidents of domestic violence, or mental, verbal, sexual abuse, or neglect involving this child, whether directly experienced or witnessed? Have you or the other parent ever been involved with law enforcement, a restraining order, protective order, or relevant medical reports? It is strongly recommended to involve law enforcement, child protective services, or medical professionals prior to filing for divorce in such situations.

____

____

____

____

Do you or the other parent have a drug or alcohol use or mental illness or anger management issue or any investigations by law enforcement or child protective services regarding this child?

____

____

____

____

Are either of the parents in a romantic relationship at this time? If so, have you observed any changes in your child?

____

____

____

____

What are any additional thoughts or considerations you have pertaining to your child and a future parenting plan agreement?

____

____

____

____

____

____

3

PARENTING PLAN IDEAS

- *Parenting Decision-Making and Responsibilities*
- *Safety Issues and "Best Interest of the Child"*
- *Communication and Information Sharing Considerations*
- *Child Custody parenting Time (Time Sharing) Arrangements*
- *Transportation of Child(ren) between Homes and Events*
- *Financial Obligations for the Benefit of the Child(ren)*
- *Other Considerations*

PARENTING PLAN IDEA WORKSHEET – SECTION 3

The Parenting Plan Idea Worksheet offers a variety of ideas and considerations. Every family is different. There may be scenarios and circumstances that you want to include in your finalized parenting plan that are specific for your situation, so feel free to change the contents or wording. Your attorney or divorce professional will draft a plan to follow your state guidelines.

A. PARENTING DECISION-MAKING AND RESPONSIBILITIES

1. Parental Decision-Making Options

Who will be making decisions on behalf of the child(ren) until they are emancipated or legal adults? There are several common options for parental decision-making post-divorce, most often referred to as joint, shared, or sole decision-making. Here are a few options for consideration. (select only one)

[ ] **Shared Parental Responsibility** – This is a good option for those who feel it is in the best interests of the child(ren) that the parents confer and **jointly** make all major decisions affecting the welfare of the child(ren). Major decisions include, but are not limited to, decisions about the child(ren)'s education, healthcare, and other responsibilities unique to this family.

[ ] **Shared Parental Responsibility with Specific Decision-Making Authority** - It is in the best interests of the child(ren) that the parents confer and attempt to agree on the major decisions involving the child(ren). If the parents are unable to agree, the authority for making major decisions regarding the child(ren) shall be as follows:

[ ] Education/Academic decisions	[ ] Mother	[ ] Father
[ ] Non-emergency health care	[ ] Mother	[ ] Father
[ ] Extracurricular activities	[ ] Mother	[ ] Father
[ ] Religious affiliation and activities	[ ] Mother	[ ] Father
[ ] ______________________________	[ ] Mother	[ ] Father
[ ] ______________________________	[ ] Mother	[ ] Father
[ ] ______________________________	[ ] Mother	[ ] Father

[ ] **Sole Parental Responsibility** - It is in the best interests of the child(ren) that the [ ] Mother [ ] Father shall have sole authority to make major decisions for the

child(ren). In my opinion, it is not in the best interest for the child(ren) to have shared parental responsibility due to the following reasons:

____

____

____

____

1. General Day-to-Day Decisions

In the event of shared custody, there are inevitably day-to-day decisions that need to be made. Some examples of day-to-day decisions are bedtimes, food choices, discipline, homework, screen time, friends, chores, allowance, responsibilities, etc. It is preferred by the courts that each household independently decide the day-to-day for their respective households. With this in mind, specific situations can be included in a parenting plan agreement when there are important items to one of the parents or if both are desiring consistency between home environments and would like to include that in the agreement. Below are some considerations on how to handle these daily decisions in a parenting agreement. (select only one)

[ ] Unless otherwise specified separately below, each parent shall make decisions regarding day-to-day care and control of each child, including the performance of daily tasks, while the child is with that parent. The day-to-day decisions include, but are not limited to, minor disciplinary actions, house rules, bedtime, homework, food choices, screen time, friends, chores, transportation, unforeseen medical emergencies, curfews, allowance and the like.

[ ] Both parties agree that the following day-to-day decisions will be handled as specified:

____

____

____

____

____

[ ] Both parties have agreed to handle the following decisions differently from each other:

____

____

____

____

____

2. Major Decision-Making Procedures

Situations with deadlines require parents to develop a system for working together efficiently. Some examples of important deadlines might include children enrolling in school by a certain date, signing up for a new healthcare plan, scheduling a medical procedure, changing classes, skipping grades, putting down a deposit for a school trip, or joining a sports team, band, or club. We strongly recommend using a co-parenting app to document the times and dates of your text, email, and phone conversations. (See ***Section 3-C:** **Communication and Information Sharing Considerations,*** for a few common options.)

Other decisions are major but **do not have a deadline** imposed by another entity. For example, picking a private tutor or music teacher, the child(ren)'s friends (for example, involvement with a friend who has committed a crime), a teen asking to go on a trip with a friend's family, a teen's request for an ear or body piercing, tattoo, birth control, an elective medical procedure, new computer, etc.

To outline the process for communication and agreement, the following options may be beneficial to include in the parenting plan agreement: (select all that apply)

For our child(ren), these decisions would be major:

____

____

____

____

[ ] For any major decisions affecting the child(ren), the parent who has become aware of the decision that needs to be made shall contact the other parent apprising him/her of the issue, the deadlines, and what preferences and rationale the parent has. The other parent shall respond to the notifying parent within______________________ (period of time) with his/her preference. This conversation should continue with the back-and-forth communication until a mutually agreeable decision is reached.

[ ] For major decisions that have a deadline set by the school or other entity, [ ] Mother [ ] Father must notify the other parent as soon as possible, but at least ____ days in advance. If the other parent fails to respond within

_____________ (period of time) of the deadline, the other parent shall make the final decision.

[ ] For decisions with no specified deadline, either parent may request an additional ______ (period of time), not to exceed ______(months) if needed, to make a decision and inform the other parent.

[ ] In the event of a disagreement over any major decision concerning the child(ren), either parent may [ ] submit the dispute to a non-binding mediation service, chosen by the parents. In the absence of an agreement a [ ] mediator, [ ] attorney [ ] other trusted representative such as a CPA or family friend or religious leader as specified ______________________ (name) may make the decision. The cost of the mediation will be [ ] shared equally [ ] paid by Mother _________% and Father_________ %.

[ ] If either parent chooses to move away_____ (miles) or further, the additional cost of transportation for child custody exchanges be handled as follows:

____

____

____

3. Decisions Regarding Education and Daycare

In the majority of situations parents will share joint legal custody, requiring educational decisions to be agreed upon by both parents. Some educational and/or daycare considerations includes items, such as where the child(ren) will attend school, access to school records, whether they will continue private school or homeschooling, emergency contacts, etc. Transportation to and from school will be addressed in a later section. (select all that apply)

[ ] Each parent shall be responsible for obtaining records and school-related information directly from the school or daycare.

[ ] Each parent shall have access to the school records and information pertaining to the child(ren) and shall be permitted to independently consult with any education or daycare professionals involved with the child(ren).

[ ] Both parents shall be listed as "emergency contacts" for the child(ren). In addition, only the following people will be added to the emergency contact list:

____

____

[ ] For purposes of K-12 school boundary determination and registration, the [ ] Mother's [ ] Father's address will be used.

[ ] The parties agree that the child(ren) will attend private school as specified, and the cost will be paid by:

____

____

____

[ ] The parties are in agreement that the child(ren) shall

[ ] continue to stay in the same school(s) or homeschool

[ ] transfer to different school(s) as specified:

____

[ ] other: ______________________________________

____

[ ] (*If Applicable*) The following provisions are made regarding private or home-schooling:

____

____

____

____

[ ] other: ______________________________________

____

4. Decisions Regarding Medical Care

Responsibility for decision-making for the child(ren) regarding medical care is also most often shared between parents. Some examples of medical considerations for a parenting plan agreement include who will provide the insurance, the decision process for following medical advice regarding medical, dental and vision care, notifications between parents and access to medical records. Parenting plan agreements often distinguish medical decisions as either routine or emergency, with different provisions and responsibilities outlined for each type of situation, in addition to high-level care decisions and information sharing. (select all that apply)

[ ] Medical insurance providing [ ] health [ ] vision and [ ] dental coverage will be provided by [ ] Mother [ ] Father. The party providing coverage will furnish all ID cards, description booklets, claim forms, login information, etc., to the other parent as often as requested to be able to use the insurance and file a claim on behalf of the child(ren).

[ ] In an effort to determine the best medical care coverage and overall benefits for the child(ren), the parents agree to review medical coverage options as follows:

[ ] review coverage options every _____ year(s)

[ ] review coverage options with every employment change

[ ] Each parent shall promptly notify the other of any significant event that affects the physical or mental welfare of the child(ren) and shall keep the other advised in advance, if possible, of any hospitalizations, surgery, medical, dental or vision treatments or examinations (except routine well-child visits and vaccinations).

[ ] Each parent shall have access to medical records and information pertaining to the child(ren) and shall be permitted to independently consult with any, and all, professionals involved with the child(ren). The parents will cooperate with each other in sharing information and shall sign any necessary documentation ensuring that both parents have access to medical records.

[ ] Other special medical conditions and responsibilities are specified below. For example, do both parents agree on routine well-child vaccinations?

____

____

____

____

Routine Medical Decision-Making

"Routine" medical refers to regularly scheduled or standard medical, dental or vision care for the child(ren). Some considerations for the handling of decision-making regarding routine medical are as follows: (select only one)

[ ] Only [ ] Mother [ ] Father may seek routine non-emergency medical treatment for the child(ren).

[ ] Each parent has the right to individually consent to and contract for routine outpatient medical, dental, or vision examinations of the child(ren) at any time during their parenting time.

[ ] Either parent may seek routine medical treatment, except for the following procedures or interventions:

____

____

____

Emergency Medical Decision-Making

Emergency medical circumstances are situations in which immediate action needs to be taken for the child(ren). In the event of such emergency medical, dental or vision care the emergency decision-making will be handled as follows: (select only one)

[ ] Either parent may seek emergency medical treatment and must inform the other parent as soon as possible regarding the situation. Either parent has the right individually to consent to and contract for emergency medical or hospital tests or treatment, including surgery, as may be necessary to preserve the life or health of the child(ren).

[ ] Either parent may seek emergency medical treatment, except for the following procedures or interventions:

____

____

____

____

Other Medical Considerations (select all that apply)

[ ] The parents agree that, to the extent reasonable and in the best interest of the child(ren), each parent will utilize healthcare providers for the child(ren) that are covered in network and under the health insurance policy.

[ ] If the child(ren) develop an ongoing medical condition or have special health

care needs, the parents will provide consistency in their care as follows (select all that apply):

[ ] The parents agree to share medical updates regarding the child(ren) as follows (select all that apply)

[ ] significant medical information related to the child(ren)

[ ] changes in medical condition of the child(ren)

[ ] other

____

____

____

____

[ ] The parent who transports the child to the other parent will ensure all medications are with the child(ren) as they travel between homes.

[ ] The following parent will fill all prescriptions and dispense medications when caring for the child(ren)? ______________________________

[ ] In cases where the parent(s) do not live close, prescription medications will be handled as follows:

____

____

[ ] Written updates will be provided for [ ] significant changes [ ] under the following circumstances:

____

____

[ ] Both parents will keep whatever physical equipment, supports or enhancements that are needed for the child(ren) in the home as specified (for example, glasses, sprints, braces, retainers, crutches, wheelchair, etc.):

____

____

[ ] The child(ren) will receive the following medical care:

____

____

[ ] The child(ren) will receive the following dental or orthodontic care:

____

____

[ ] The child(ren) will receive the following vision care:

____

____

[ ] Both parents agree that the child(ren) will undergo psychiatric or other mental health care in the following situations: (select all that apply)

[ ] if either parent feels it is necessary

[ ] only if agreed on by both parents in writing

[ ] if it is recommended by a school counselor or other health care professional

[ ] only if it is available at a low or no cost option as specified

____

____

[ ] other

____

____

[ ] If it is deemed in the best interest of the child(ren), the parents agree to personally undergo psychiatric or other mental health care in the following situations: (select all that apply)

[ ] if either parent feels it is necessary

[ ] if it is recommended by a school counselor or other health care professional

[ ] only if it is available at a low or no cost option as specified

____

[ ] other

____

[ ] If currently recommended by a pediatrician or mental health professional, or recommended in the future, both parents agree that the child(ren) may take the following medications, dose, and frequency, as prescribed by a physician and listed below:

[ ] Child ____
Medication(s) ____

[ ] Child ____
Medication(s) ____

[ ] Child ____
Medication(s) ____

[ ] Child ____
Medication(s) ____

[ ] The child(ren) will receive the following mental health care, monthly or weekly or as needed.

____

____

____

____

5. Decisions Regarding Extracurricular Activities and Camps

Extracurricular activities (for example, sports, theater, music, camps, etc.) are unique to each family and often to each child within a family. The scheduling and transportation for activities outside the home can become even more complicated during a separation or divorce. New factors will likely need to be considered for post-divorce life, such as if the activity might impact the other parent's parenting time. Below are some of the options that you may want to consider including in a parenting plan agreement to facilitate coordination and clarity around the co-parenting roles and responsibilities.

Activity Scheduling Constraints (select only one)

[ ] Either parent may register the child(ren) and allow them to participate in the activities of the child(ren)'s choice that *solely impact their own parenting time*. No activity can be scheduled that impacts the other party's parenting time without their written consent in advance.

[ ] The parents agree that either parent may register the child(ren) and allow them to participate in activities of the child(ren)'s choice, *regardless of whose parenting time the activity may impact*.

Activity Transportation

There are several ways to handle the transportation of the child(ren) to and from extracurricular activities. Below are some options to consider. (select only one)

[ ] The parent who signed up the child(ren) for the extracurricular activity will provide all transportation for that activity.

[ ] The parent who has parenting time with the child(ren) at the time of the scheduled extracurricular activity shall transport the child(ren) to and from all agreed upon extracurricular activities during their parenting time.

[ ] Transportation for the child(ren)'s activities will be handled as follows:

____

____

____

____

Activity Costs

As finances and money may become contentious during and after divorce, it may be helpful to explicitly define how the costs associated with extracurricular activities and camps will be handled. Below are some options to consider.

[ ] The parent who signed up the child(ren) for the extracurricular activity will pay all expenses for that activity, including transportation.

[ ] The parents agree that all the registration fees, equipment, uniforms, transportation, and all the expenses will be handled as follows: (select one)

[ ] divided based on the current income Mother _______% Father ______%

[ ] divided with Mother _______% Father _______%.

[ ] The parents agree to split the registration fees, equipment, uniforms, transportation, and all the expenses as follows:

Activity: _________________________ Mother _______% Father _______%
Activity: _________________________ Mother _______% Father _______%
Activity: _________________________ Mother _______% Father _______%
Activity: _________________________ Mother _______% Father _______%
Activity: _________________________ Mother _______% Father _______%
Activity: _________________________ Mother _______% Father _______%
Activity: _________________________ Mother _______% Father _______%
Activity: _________________________ Mother _______% Father _______%

[ ] Extraordinary Costs. The parents agree to split the expenses of extraordinary cost associated with extracurricular activities such as uniforms, musical instruments, vehicles, horses, safety equipment, etc., as follows:

Expense: _________________________ Mother _______% Father _______%
Expense: _________________________ Mother _______% Father _______%
Expense: _________________________ Mother _______% Father _______%
Expense: _________________________ Mother _______% Father _______%
Expense: _________________________ Mother _______% Father _______%
Expense: _________________________ Mother _______% Father _______%
Expense: _________________________ Mother _______% Father _______%
Expense: _________________________ Mother _______% Father _______%

Other Extracurricular Activity Options (select all that apply)

[ ] The following will be the procedure if essential items are forgotten at the other parent's house for an extracurricular activity, such as, but not limited to, medication, special equipment, uniforms, shoes, costumes, musical instruments, safety gear, school projects and other such items:

____
____
____

[ ] The child(ren) <u>may</u> participate in the following extracurricular activities (list activities and explain):

____
____
____
____

[ ] The child(ren) <u>may not</u> participate in the following extracurricular activities (list activities and explain):

____
____
____
____

[ ] Camps and/or extracurricular activities involving multiple nights away from family should not exceed ______________ (time period) until the child(ren) are ____________ (age), unless otherwise agreed in writing between co-parents.

[ ] Camps and/or extracurricular activities with multiple overnights away from home will be handled as follows:

____
____
____
____

[ ] Camps and/or extracurricular activities involving out-of-area travel will be handled as follows:

____
____
____
____

[ ] Other agreements concerning extracurricular activities and explain:

____

____

____

____

B. Safety and the Best Interest of the Child(ren)

While both parents must follow state regulations regarding child safety equipment and protection (for example, car seats, bike helmets, etc.), there may be additional parameters you would like to include in the parenting plan agreement in the best interest and safety of the child(ren). (select all that apply)

[ ] Both parents agree to restrict child(ren)'s access to the following without written consent from the other parent: [ ] ATVs [ ] motorcycles [ ] snowmobiles [ ] bungee jumping [ ] parachuting [ ] other activities listed below:

____

____

[ ] The [ ] Mother [ ] Father [ ] other party _______________________ (name) may not consume alcoholic beverages, narcotics, or restricted drugs (except by prescription) within_________ hours before or during periods of time with the children and [ ] may [ ] may not allow any third party to do so in the presence of the child(ren). If the other parent's drug or alcohol use or anger management issues are a problem, see ***Section 4: Joint Custody Considerations.***

[ ] The [ ] Mother [ ] Father [ ] other party _______________________ (name) may not watch or expose child(ren) to any pornography while with children and may not allow any third party to do so in the presence of the child(ren).

[ ] The parents agree they will not expose the child(ren) to secondhand cigarette, vaping and medical or recreational marijuana smoke.

[ ] Both parents agree to ensure all prescriptions drugs and firearms are safely stored and out of reach of the child(ren) in the following manner:

____

____

____

[ ] Unless specified by a separate state regulation, the child(ren) must not be left alone before the age of _________ (specify age) without age-appropriate supervision, which is defined as:

____

____

____

[ ] The child(ren) will have no contact with the following people:

____

____

____

[ ] The child(ren) may not be left alone in the presence of:

____

____

____

[ ] The child(ren) [ ] may [ ] may not attend slumber parties or sleepovers at the following individuals' homes and/or under the following circumstances:

____

____

____

[ ] Both parents agree to use software to :

[ ] filter/block explicit content
[ ] filter/block violent content
[ ] block or de-install applications as noted below
[ ] monitor time spent on the computer the child(ren)'s electronic devices

____

____

[ ] Both parents agree to other arrangements and/or regarding the child(ren)'s devices as follows:

____

____

____

[ ] In the best interest of our minor child(ren): (select all that apply)

[ ] Both parents agree that the child(ren) have the right to love both parents.

Both parents will make efforts to support the child(ren)'s desire to communicate with and have a warm relationship with the other parent.

[ ] Both parents agree to refrain from hostility toward the other parent in front of the child(ren) and will not attempt to influence the child(ren) unfavorably toward the other parent.

[ ] Both parents agree to not use religious condemnation to influence the child(ren)'s view of the other parent.

[ ] The parents agree to describe the reason for the divorce/separation to their minor child(ren) using the following phrase or explanation:

____

____

____

____

[ ] If asked by the child(ren) about the divorce/separation, the parents agree to use their best judgment and refrain from any disparaging comments.

[ ] Both parents agree to not say anything disparaging about the other parent until the child is over [ ] 18 years [ ] _______ (age) and specifically asks.

[ ] Other than age-appropriate discussions of the parenting plan agreement and the child(ren)'s role in mediation or other court proceedings, the parents will not discuss with the children any court proceedings relating to custody or parenting-time/visitation until the age of _______ (specify age). Please check this with your attorney. Note: Some courts do not want parenting plans discussed with children.

[ ] Both parents agree to not use any electronics, devices, GPS, software, or any other method to eavesdrop, surveil, wiretap, or track the child(ren), or other parent, except as agreed below:

____

____

____

[ ] It is requested that the other parent be restricted to monitored visitation with the child(ren) and no unsupervised visits due to the following reason:

____

____

____

[ ] Other agreements in the best interest and safety of the child(ren):

____

____

____

____

C. COMMUNICATION AND INFORMATION SHARING CONSIDERATIONS:

Communication between parents of shared child(ren) is extremely important during and following divorce, but can be difficult in some situations. This can be especially true if there are angry or hurt feelings over the separation or divorce. Likewise, a high-conflict divorce creates even more challenges with communication and information sharing. Regardless of any ill-feelings or conflicts, it is likely that both parents will want and need information about the child(ren), whether it is regarding health care, school, outside activities, new developments, interests, etc. When considering communication and information sharing on the parenting plan agreement, it is important to try to address everyone's needs. Communication styles may differ based on the level of conflict or amicability between the parents, so keep this in mind when considering options for your agreement. Ultimately, the most important thing is to ensure both parents are getting the appropriate information and that the child(ren) are not being used as communication channels between the parents. This puts the child(ren) in the middle which has been proven to be emotionally harmful for them and may even stifle or delay their adaptation during and after the separation or divorce.

1. Communication and Information Sharing Between Parents (select all that apply)

[ ] Both parents agree to communicate directly to one another and not ask the children to pass messages, ask questions, gather information, spy, or make schedule changes unless it's an emergency.

[ ] The parents agree to: (select all that apply)

[ ] communicate every __________ (time period) at ______________ (location) to review information pertaining to the child(ren)'s development, school, health, activities and any other information important to share.

[ ] The parents shall communicate with each other through the following options (select all that apply)

[ ] In person
[ ] By telephone
[ ] By letter
[ ] By e-mail
[ ] By text
[ ] Through a co-parenting app [ ] OurFamilyWizard [ ] AppClose [ ] Civil Communicator [ ] TalkingParents [ ] Other App ____________________
[ ] Other ____

[ ] Other agreements regarding communication and information sharing between parents:

____
____
____
____

2. **Communication and Information Sharing Between Parent and Child(ren)** (select all that apply)

[ ] Communication between the child(ren) and one parent shall not be monitored by, or interrupted by, the other parent [ ] ever [ ] after age _________.

[ ] The child(ren) may have [ ] telephone [ ] e-mail [ ] other electronic contact with the other parent as follows: (various options)

[ ] Anytime
[ ] Every day during the hours of______________ to ____________________
[ ] On the following days____
during the hours of ______________________ to ____________________
[ ] Only in case of emergency
[ ] Only for ___________ (length of time)
[ ] Other:____

[ ] It is a parent's responsibility to reach out to the child. The other parent will encourage the children to maintain contact, if the child wishes, and will provide a means of communicating with the other parent (phone, computer, etc.) as

follows: (select all that apply)

[ ] Daily as specified (during what hours)

____

____

[ ] Weekly as specified:

____

____

[ ] During vacations as specified:

____

____

[ ] Whenever the child(ren) requests the parent to call, as specified:

____

____

[ ] If the child is busy or away from the phone when the parent calls and the parent leaves a message, the child will:

[ ] be played the parent's message (age ______ to ______)

[ ] be encouraged to call the other parent back in the next 24 hours, given privacy and use of a phone or computer (if age appropriate), and leave a message if there is no answer

[ ] be provided with a phone and decide for themselves whether to call back or not (starting at age ______)

[ ] Other

____

____

____

____

____

3. Costs of Electronic Communication

The associated cost of electronic communication between parent and child(ren) shall be addressed as follows ("Electronic communication" includes telephones, smart watches, text messaging, e-mail, webcams, video-conferencing equipment, or other means of communication to supplement face-to-face contact):

____

____

____

____

4. Changes in Address, Phone and Other Information Sharing and Access (select all that apply)

[ ] Each parent has a continuing responsibility to provide a residential, mailing, and contact address and contact telephone number, both home and mobile, and email, to the other parent. Each parent shall notify the other parent in writing within 24 hours of any changes.

[ ] Both parents must notify the other parent within ______ days before any changes in [ ] residency [ ] mailing [ ] work [ ] e-mail [ ] phone(s).

[ ] Both parents must inform the other parent of any changes to the telephone number at [ ] home [ ] work [ ] mobile. Neither parent may use such information for the purposes of harassing, annoying or disturbing the peace of the other parent or invading the other's privacy. No residence or address is necessary to disclose if protected by a law enforcement or government confidential address program.

[ ] Both parents shall have equal and independent authority to confer with the child(ren)'s professional service providers, such as doctors or therapists, or with their school with regard to the child(ren)'s educational, emotional, and social progress.

[ ] The parents agree to provide to the other parent information related to the health, education and welfare issues that arise during the time the child(ren) are in their care:

[ ] yes [ ] no

If yes, the parents agree to:

[ ] maintain a "log book" and make sure that the book is sent with the child(ren) between homes
[ ] Use business-like notes only (no personal comments)
[ ] Other:____

[ ] If either parent moves to another country, they will pay for a security child custody bond to ensure payment of child and spousal support and the return of the child(ren) following a visit.

[ ] Other agreements regarding communication or information sharing:
____
____
____
____
____
____
____

D. CHILD CUSTODY / PARENTING TIME ARRANGEMENTS

The term child custody is typically used in separation or divorce to define the physical time each parent spends with the child(ren). The terminology is commonly used in legal documents often with a broader definition than just physical time. That said, many states are moving away from the terms "custody" and "visitation," moving instead towards other wording, with the most common being "child custody," "parenting time," "parenting responsibilities" and "time-sharing".

Every state has guidelines for child support and child custody. Not surprisingly, the calculation of child support paid often correlates with the percentage of time the child spends with each parent. Keep in mind that the last thing your child(ren) wants is to feel like a possession being divided between parents for financial reasons. For a better understanding of the child support/alimony determinations for your specific state, search online for your state's child support guidelines. Many states even have a free calculator on-line to determine the specific amounts to be awarded based on income and percentage of time with each parent.

1. Do an online search for the phrase: "child support calculator for [your state]" OR "spousal support calculator for [your state]".
2. Fill in the form to the best of your ability and see what the online calculator determines as the approximate support payment based on the information you've provided.
3. For advice on your personal situation, consult with your attorney or legal professional for additional questions or clarifications.

When it comes to parenting plan agreements, one of the most common oversights is not factoring in the evolving needs of the child(ren) over time. Children adjust best when they have decision-making ability and increasing responsibility for their own lives. Consider divorces that occur when the children are young. Agreements that worked for a toddler don't work well for middle schoolers or teens. For example, infants may need greater time with the mother than they might when they turn 5 years old. Another oversight is not building flexibility into the plan for teenagers, giving them more autonomy and flexibility in their schedules as they want their own transportation and grow closer to adulthood. They have their own friends and activities, and if parenting time impinges on their friendships and school activities, they may grow resentful. Regardless of age, try your best to see the time-sharing arrangement through the eyes of your child(ren) and how it might feel at various ages. Lastly, your attorney, mediator, or legal professional can provide specific guidance on what is acceptable in your state for your individual case.

1. Custody/Parenting Time Arrangement Options

While there may be other applicable ways to define the physical time with the child(ren), sole and shared custody are the most common arrangement.
(select only one)

[ ] **Sole Physical Custody**. [ ] Mother [ ] Father will have sole physical custody of the child(ren). (This is not typical in most states unless one parent has been convicted of a crime, does not want custody, or cannot physically care for the child(ren) due to their job or for some other reason.)

[ ] **Shared Physical Custody**. The parties shall share physical custody and parenting time with the child(ren).

WHAT IS THE BEST INTEREST OF THE CHILD? KNOW THE "HOLLEY FACTORS"

Some courts may use the "Holley Factors" or similar guidelines when deciding what is in the child(ren)'s best interest. The court wants to know how the child(ren) have been cared for in the past, and what is sensible for the future.

- **Physical and Emotional Needs** Which parent will best provide for the child(ren)'s physical, psychological, and emotional needs, and development now and in the future.
- **Physical and Emotional Danger** Whether either parent poses any physical or emotional danger to the child(ren) now or in the future.
- **False Report of Child Abuse** Whether either parent ever knowingly made a false report of child abuse. If the court finds that a report of child abuse is false *or lacking factual foundation,* the court may restrict further access to the child by the parent who made the report. (Note: Research by law professor Joan S. Meier, of George Washington University, has shown the sad reality of court bias against mothers who make abuse allegations (with or without evidence), and found they may lose custody themselves.)
- **Stability of Home** Stability of each parent's home.
- **Plans for the Child** Each parent's plans for the child(ren), e.g., living arrangement, education, after-school care, extracurricular activities, etc.
- **Cooperation Between Parents** Each parent's ability to give the child(ren) priority and reach shared decisions in the child(ren)'s best interest.
- **Parenting Skills** Each parent's parenting skills.
- **Primary Caregiver** Which parent was the child(ren)'s primary caregiver before the divorce.
- **Child's Preferences** Ask your attorney whether your child's preference factors into the court's decision in your state or jurisdiction. Some courts do not want the parents to ask the child(ren) for fear the parent will try to influence them.
- **Geographic Proximity** Where the parents currently reside (if separated), or plan to reside, in relation to each other.
- **Siblings** If divided or split conservatorship is requested, the effect separation would have on the siblings.
- **Promoting Relationships Between the Child(ren) and Other Parent** The extent to which each parent can encourage and accept a positive relationship between the child(ren) and the other parent.
- **International Child Abduction** The need for measures to protect the child(ren) from being internationally abducted to a foreign country.

- **Present Fitness and Recent Past Conduct** Each parent's present fitness to care for the child(ren), and the recent past conduct of each parent, as a reasonable predictor of the parent's behavior in the future.
- **Drug or Alcohol Abuse:** A parent having a drug or alcohol problem. A parent may be denied managing conservatorship based on recent drug or alcohol abuse.
- **Sexual Conduct** A parent's sexual conduct to the extent that it renders that parent unfit to act as a parent. This generally pertains to illegal conduct (pedophilia, etc.), not to having adult romantic partners stay overnight.

The following factors are factors that the Court may not consider when determining the best interest of the child(ren): Gender, Race, Religion, Immigration status, Marital status (when modifying custody cases brought after divorce).

2. Weekend and Weekday Schedule

Once sole or shared custody has been decided, the next step is to decide on a schedule for the child(ren). Many different scheduling arrangements are possible, for example, one week on/one week off, every other weekend, etc. Likewise, time-sharing may differ for each child as the needs of each individual child may be more conducive to different arrangements. For a detailed look at some sample time-sharing schedules, review ***Section 5 Time-Sharing Scheduling and Sample Calendars*** in this workbook. If time-sharing differs for each child, the individual schedules should be separately defined in the parenting agreement. (select only one)

The following schedule shall apply beginning on________________________(date) with the [ ] Mother [ ] Father and continue as follows:

a. The child(ren) shall spend time with the **Mother** on the following dates and times:
WEEKENDS: [ ] Every [ ] Every Other [ ] Other (specify) ____________________
from__________________________________
to ___________________________________
WEEKDAYS: specify days ____
from__________________________________
to ___________________________________
OTHER: (specify) ____

b. The child(ren) shall spend time with the **Father** on the following dates and times:

WEEKENDS: [ ] Every [ ] Every Other [ ] Other (specify) ____________________

from__________________________________

to ___________________________________

WEEKDAYS: specify days ____

from__________________________________

to ___________________________________

OTHER: (specify) ____

The following chart can be used to fill in with either Mother/Father based on the planned overnight schedule. Refer to ***Section 5: Time-Sharing Scheduling and Sample Calendars.***

	Sunday	Monday	Tuesday	Wednesday	Thursday	Friday	Saturday
Week 1							
Week 2							
Week 3							
Week 4							

[ ] Based upon the time-sharing schedule, the Mother has a total of _____ overnights per year and the Father has a total of _____ overnights per year. **Note:** For shared custody the two numbers must equal 365 (or 366 in a leap year).

3. Holidays and Special Dates Schedule

There may be several approaches on how to handle the scheduling of holidays and special dates. Below are a few options for consideration: (select only one)

[ ] No holiday time-sharing shall apply. The regular time-sharing schedule defined above shall apply regardless of holidays or special dates.

[ ] The parents agree to a separate holiday schedule which will take priority over the regular weekday, weekend, and summer schedules.

[ ] Holiday time-sharing shall be as the parties agree and specify below:

____

____

____

____

In the event of a separate holiday schedule (as selected above), fill in the following grid with Mother or Father to indicate where the child(ren) will be for the specific holidays or special dates. Providing the beginning and ending times is a good practice as it helps eliminates confusion as to when the exchange is to occur. It is common for parenting plans to define years as “Even” or “Odd” and split the time accordingly. If a holiday is not specified as even/odd or every other year with one parent, then the child(ren) will remain with the parent in accordance with the regular time-sharing schedule.

Holidays	**Even Years?**	**Odd Years?**	**Every Year?**	**Who Transports / Holiday Start Time?**	**Who Transports / Holiday End Time?**
Example - Easter	*Mom*	*Dad*		*Mother / 7:00 am*	*Father / 8:00 pm*
New Year’s Day					
MLK Birthday Weekend					
Chinese New Year					
Easter					
Passover					
President’s Day Weekend					
Ramadan					
Mother’s Day					
Memorial Day Weekend					
Father’s Day					
4th Of July					
Labor Day Weekend					
Rosh Hashanah					
Columbus Day Weekend					
Halloween					
Veterans Day					
Thanksgiving Day					
Thanksgiving Weekend					
Hanukkah					
Yom Kippur					

Christmas Eve					
Christmas					
New Year's Eve					
Other					

a. **Child(ren)'s Birthdays** (select only one)

[ ] Every other year, the child will spend their actual birthday alternating between the two parents.

[ ] The child(ren)'s birthday will be spent with the parent who has regularly scheduled parenting time falling on that date.

[ ] The child(ren)'s actual birthday will always be spent with the [ ] Mother [ ] Father.

[ ] Other: ____
____
____
____
____

b. **Spring Break** Options (select only one):

[ ] The parents shall follow the regular time-sharing schedule through Spring Break.

[ ] The [ ] Mother [ ] Father shall have the child(ren) from the day and time school is dismissed for Spring Break _____ at ___ a.m./p.m. until
[ ] the Friday before school starts
[ ] after school on the day the child(ren) go back to school

This schedule will occur on

[ ] odd-numbered years
[ ] even-numbered years
[ ] every year
[ ] the parties will alternate the arrangement each year

[ ] The Spring Break will be divided as follows:

____
____
____
____

[ ] Other: ____

____
____
____
____

c. Summer Break Options (select only one):

[ ] The parents shall follow the regular time-sharing schedule through Summer Break.

[ ] The child(ren) will spend the entire Summer Break with [ ] Mother [ ] Father starting from _________ (days) after school is out until _________ (days) before school starts.

[ ] The Summer Break will be evenly divided. During [ ] odd-numbered years or [ ] even numbered years, the [ ] Mother [ ] Father shall have the children from ________ (date) after school is out until ________ (date). The other parent shall have the child(ren) for the second one-half of the Summer Break. The parents shall alternate the first and second one-halves each year unless otherwise agreed.

[ ] The Summer Break will be divided as follows:

____
____

____

____

[ ] Other: ____

____

____

____

____

d. Fall Break Options (choose only one):

[ ] The parents shall follow the regular time-sharing schedule through Fall Break.

[ ] The [ ] Mother [ ] Father shall have the child(ren) from the day and time school is dismissed for Fall Break _____ at ___ a.m./p.m. until

[ ] the Friday before school starts
[ ] after school on the day the child(ren) go back to school

This schedule will occur on

[ ] odd-numbered years
[ ] even-numbered years
[ ] every year
[ ] the parties will alternate the arrangement each year

[ ] The Fall Break will be divided as follows:

____

____

____

____

[ ] Other: ____

____

____

____

____

e. Winter Break Options (select only one):

[ ] The parents shall follow the regular time-sharing schedule through Winter Break.

[ ] The [ ] Mother [ ] Father shall have the child(ren) from the day and time school is dismissed for Winter Break ______ at ___ a.m./p.m. until

[ ] the Friday before school starts
[ ] after school on the day the child(ren) go back to school

This schedule will occur on

[ ] odd-numbered years
[ ] even-numbered years
[ ] every year
[ ] the parties will alternate the arrangement each year
[ ] the Winter Break will be <u>evenly</u> divided as follows:

____

____

[ ] The Winter Break will be divided as follows:

____

____

____

____

[ ] Other: ____

____

____

____

____

3. Vacations During Regular Time-Sharing

Vacations are special trips planned with the child(ren) that take place separate from school breaks, holidays and special dates as outlined above. For example, a parent may want to take a travel vacation with the child(ren) over the summer.

When considering vacation time, the first objective is to determine when this additional time will be allowable for the parents. (select only one)

[ ] Neither party is allowed to take vacations with minor children outside of the allocated regular time-sharing, holiday, and school break schedules. All vacation time must use the parent's own parenting time so as to not interfere with the other parent's time with the child(ren).

[ ] Each party is entitled to take vacations with minor children for up to _________ [ ] days [ ] weeks per vacation trip even if the vacation interferes with the other co-parent's parenting time.

After establishing the high-level agreement on vacation time outside of regularly scheduled parenting time and the holiday schedule, additional specifications can be made regarding the vacation time with the child(ren). (select all that apply)

[ ] The vacation time [ ] may [ ] may not last more than ____ consecutive days.

[ ] The vacation time [ ] may [ ] may not cause the child(ren) to miss school without written consent of the other parent.

[ ] The parent planning the vacation with the child(ren) will give the other parent ______ days' notice.

[ ] By _____________ (date) of each year, the parties agree to provide advance notice to each other of all intended vacations and provide an itinerary, including contact information, __________ (number of days) prior to such travel.

[ ] Any vacation that conflicts with the other parent's parenting time needs written approval from the impacted parent. The request should be made, in writing (specifying dates and locations), a minimum of _________ (number of days) in advance. The impacted parent must approve or deny the request, in writing, a maximum of ________ (number of days) from the requested approval date. If approval is not received by this time, the requested vacation will be handled as follows:

____

____

____

____

____

____

[ ] Bereavement: In the case of the [ ] imminent death [ ] death of immediate family (father, mother, siblings, spouse, stepparent, in-laws, grandparents) [ ] death of immediate family or significant individuals listed below, the parent may take the child for _________ (number of days), provided the other parent was notified at least _________ (number of days) in advance. The bereaved parent will reimburse the other parent for any non-refundable fees of pre-paid events that were impacted due to the changes in overnights according to the regular expense reimbursement requirements.

Bereavement List of other significant individuals, who are not immediate family to the child, for example a special classmate or teacher:

____

____

____

____

____

____

____

____

4. Impacts to the Regular Scheduled Parenting Time

Holidays and vacations can sometimes affect the regular agreed-upon time-sharing schedule. Due to this, parents may wish to specify one or more of the following options:

[ ] When the parents are using an alternating weekend plan (see sample calendars in ***Section 5***), and the holiday schedule would result in one parent having the child(ren) for three weekends in a row, the parents will exchange the following weekend, so that each has two weekends in a row before the regular alternating weekend pattern resumes.

[ ] If a parent has the child(ren) on a weekend immediately before or after an unspecified holiday (a holiday not specified in the agreement) or non-school day (for example, a teacher resource day), the parent with the regularly scheduled parenting time shall have the child(ren) for that holiday or non-school day.

[ ] With regards to overnights, the rotations following a vacation/holiday schedule

will [ ] remain unchanged [ ] will alternate such that the non-vacationing parent can be with the child(ren) the following weekend upon return.

5. Vacation/Travel Conflicts

There may be occasions where one parent's planned vacation or travel arrangement conflicts with the other parent's plans. For example, both parents may have planned to take a travel vacation with the child(ren) for one week in the summer, only to find out that their trips overlap. The following is an option that can be included in the parenting plan arrangement to help mitigate this issue. (select only one)

[ ] In the event that the parents' dates of travel are in conflict
[ ] Mother's [ ] Father's travel plans will have priority.

[ ] In the event that the parents' dates of travel are in conflict, Mother's travel plans will have priority in the [ ] Even [ ] Odd years and Father's travel plans will have priority in the [ ] Even [ ] Odd years.

6. Other Travel Considerations

Below are some additional travel considerations that may be beneficial to add to the parenting plan agreement. (select all that apply)

[ ] The parents agree that either parent may travel with the child(ren) anywhere <u>within the United States</u> during his/her time-sharing as follows:
(select only one)

[ ] The parent may travel <u>without</u> the verbal or written permission from the other parent.

[ ] The parent may travel only <u>with</u> explicit written permission from the other parent.

[ ] Either parent may travel <u>out of the country</u> with the child(ren) during his/her time-sharing with written permission from the other parent. (See the next section for other passport issues)

[ ] Each parent agrees to cooperate with the passport process as well as expeditiously sign whatever documentation is necessary for the other parent to take the child(ren) out of the country.

[ ] The parent traveling with the child(ren) to another state or country shall give the other parent at least ______ days written notice before traveling and shall provide the other parent with a detailed itinerary, including locations and telephone numbers where the child(ren) and parent can be reached. This information will be provided at least ______ days before departure.

[ ] If a parent wishes to travel out of the country with the child(ren), they shall:

[ ] return the child(ren) within ________ (number of days)
[ ] provide the following security (for example, a child custody bond) for the return of the child(ren):

____

____

____

[ ] If parents are unable to agree on vacation plans or specifications, they will contact the following to resolve the conflict:

[ ] dispute resolution specialist / mediator
[ ] attorney(s)
[ ] mutually trusted friend, religious leader, or other trusted person(s) listed here to resolve the conflict:

____

____

____

[ ] Other agreements regarding travel:

____

____

____

____

7. Child(ren)'s Passports

While most parents cooperate and view international travel as a wonderful education and family-bonding experience, there may be cases where there is a flight risk or the possibility of international child abduction. In these situations, it may be helpful to add some restrictions around the supervision and/or possession of the passports for the child(ren). For example, for U.S. citizens, programs like the *Children's Passport Issuance Alert Program* may be necessary (see link below). Even if child abduction is not a concern, additional foreign travel securities may still be prudent and worth considering. Below are some examples. (select all that apply)

Children's Passport Issuance Alert Program Link:
https://travel.state.gov/content/travel/en/International-Parental-Child-Abduction/prevention/passport-issuance-alert-program.html.

[ ] Passports will be held by (select only one)

[ ] Mother [ ] Father will be the sole holder of the child(ren)'s passports.

[ ] The passports will be held between both parents with Mother holding the following child(ren)'s passports

____

and Father holding the following child(ren)'s passports

____

[ ] A third party will hold the child(ren)'s passports as specified:

____

[ ] The parents agree that neither parent shall unreasonably withhold the child(ren)'s passports from the other parent.

[ ] Both parents shall be given photocopies of the children's passports as well as each a photocopy of each other's current passports and provide new copies within_________ (number of months) of any renewal or replacement.

[ ] Due to a flight risk, the court order will be shared with other consulates requesting that no foreign passports are issued to the children if the other parent is a citizen of another country.

[ ] A request will be made with the U.S. State Department not to allow the children a visa to be issued for another country.

[ ] The child(ren) will be registered with the Department of State's Children's Passport Issuance Alert Program.

[ ] If a parent wishes to travel out of the country with the child(ren), he/she should provide the following security (e.g. child custody bond, vehicles, real estate, etc.) for the return of the child(ren) within ________ (number of days):

____

____

____

8. Other Time-Sharing Considerations

Childcare, school calendar variations, and schedule interruptions are all examples of areas where additional clarification can be built into the parenting plan agreement to support a stress-free situation post-divorce.

Childcare (select all that apply)

[ ] Each parent may select childcare providers of their own choice.

[ ] All childcare providers must be agreed upon by both parents.

[ ] First right of Refusal. Each parent must offer the other parent the opportunity to care for the child(ren) before using a childcare provider for any overnight or period exceeding _________ hours. The other parent has ________ (number of hours) to respond.

[ ] Other: ____

____

____

____

School Calendar (select all that apply)

[ ] If necessary, on or before ______________(date) of each year, both parents are individually responsible to obtain a copy of the school calendar for the next school year and discuss the calendars and time-sharing schedule so that any conflicts or questions can be resolved. (School districts often post their calendars online.)

[ ] The parents shall follow the school calendar of: (Choose all that apply)

[ ] The oldest child
[ ] The youngest child
[ ] The school calendar for ________________________ (county)
[ ] The school calendar for ________________________ (school)
[ ] Other as specified:

____

____

Schedule Interruptions and Changes

It is almost certain that unexpected circumstances will arise that require interruptions to the regular, agreed upon time-sharing arrangement in which the parent responsible for the child(ren) will not be available during their regularly scheduled parenting time. Some examples include a sickness or injury impacting a parent's ability to have the child(ren), a sudden business trip, a parent being called away due to a family emergency, work emergency, or military or National Guard service, etc. For example, if one parent was scheduled to have the child from Feb 2nd to Feb 9th, but their boss makes a last-minute demand that they fly to another state on Feb 7th, are the timesharing hours with the children forfeited, or do the parents make a trade for the time if convenient? The following are some considerations for the parenting plan agreement to handle these schedule interruptions or changes. (select all that apply)

[ ] FOR UNFORESEEN EMERGENCIES: A parent making a request for an emergency schedule change will make the request to the other parent immediately, via the method(s) selected below, before the interruption is to occur. The other parent will respond in a timely fashion, or at least within ______ hours, otherwise it is the requesting parent's responsibility to find a workaround.

[ ] phone call
[ ] email
[ ] text message
[ ] other as specified:

____

____

[ ] NON-EMERGENCY: A parent making a request for a schedule change will make the request to the other parent a soon as possible, via the method(s) selected below. This should take place no less than ________________ (hours/days)

before the interruption is to occur. The parent being asked to cover, can agree to trade time, but is not obligated to do so. They can also decline if the schedule change would be inconvenient. It is the responsibility of the requesting party to find alternative arrangements.

[ ] phone call
[ ] email
[ ] text message
[ ] other as specified:

____

____

[ ] A parent requesting a change of schedule shall be responsible for any additional childcare, transportation, or other costs incurred by the parent making the request.

[ ] Parenting time lost due to the interruption [ ] will be [ ] will not be replaced with time from subsequent time-sharing. If it will be made up, the replacement time must be substituted within ______________ (timeframe).

[ ] Other:

____

____

____

____

First Right of Refusal for Missed Overnights

The first right of refusal clause is common in some states and refers to a statement in the agreement to specify that if the parent is unable to spend his/her regularly scheduled parenting time with the child(ren), the other parent has the right to be asked first to care for the child(ren), prior to any third party (such as a grandparent or babysitter). This situation could happen voluntarily or due to unforeseen circumstances. In either case, the objective of the clause it to give the other parent the opportunity to have the time with the child(ren) prior to anyone else.
(select only one)

[ ] In the event that one parent is unable to exercise their parenting time overnight(s), that parent shall offer the overnight(s) missed of parenting time to

the other parent before any third party. In the event the other parent is unable or unwilling to provide care, it is the responsibility of the parent with the scheduled time to arrange and pay for appropriate childcare.

[ ] In the event that one parent is unable to exercise their parenting time overnight(s), that parent shall offer the overnight(s) to the other parent OR these specific trusted individuals (i.e., grandparents, aunts, uncles, family friend) to provide care. It is the responsibility of the parent with the scheduled parenting time to arrange and pay for the appropriate childcare if none of these individuals are available.

[ ] List of trusted individuals:

____

____

____

[ ] List of unacceptable individuals:

____

____

____

[ ] List of acceptable childcare centers:

____

____

____

[ ] List of acceptable childcare providers/options for sick children:

____

____

____

[ ] Other agreements regarding missed parenting time:

____

____

____

____

E. TRANSPORTATION OF CHILD(REN) BETWEEN HOMES AND EVENTS

A sign of good cooperation between parents is the well-organized and drama-free transition from one home to the other. Moving between homes requires repeated emotional, logistical, and physical preparation. Put yourselves in your child's shoes when considering the parenting plan agreement. Even in the best organized home, the stress of getting the homework, school supplies, lunches, stuffed animals, sports equipment, medications, mobile phones, hygiene items, and other belongings can be taxing to kids and parents alike. The concept of "nesting," which eliminates the need for the child(ren) to move back and forth, is gaining popularity in amicable divorces where the right circumstances exist for this option. "Nesting" means that the child(ren) stay in the home, and the parents spend their parenting time living there (including overnights) and returning to their separate homes when their parenting time is over. Nesting can also be used as a interim phase during separation as the parents go through the divorce process. Nesting is not always financially feasible, since three homes are being maintained.

Types of Child(ren) Exchanges and Arrangements (select only one)

[ ] The parents have agreed to a nesting arrangement, where the children remain in the [family home] or [other home]. The parents each have their own separate homes but stay with the children in the family home during their designated parenting time.

____

____

[ ] The child(ren) will be transferred between the parents' individual homes.

[ ] Other arrangements:

____

____

____

____

____

Exchange Location (select only one)

[ ] The exchanges shall take place at [ ] Mother's home [ ] Father's home [ ] other, as specified below, unless both parents agree in advance in writing,

text, or email to a different meeting place:

____

____

[ ] The exchanges shall take place at the home of the parent whose parenting time is starting, unless otherwise agreed upon in advance in writing, text or email for a different arrangement. For example, if Mother's parenting time is starting, the Father is responsible for dropping off the child with important, agreed upon items, such as backpack, medication, hygiene products, uniforms, etc. To avoid misunderstandings, a list of specific items can be created in the next section.

[ ] The exchanges will take place at a [ ] fast-food restaurant [ ] fire station [ ] trusted friend/family member's home [ ] half-way between residences at a certain location [ ] other as specified below:

(Often a public place with security cameras can be a good option. Police stations are generally frowned upon now due to the negative connotation possibly suggesting that one parent is a criminal. A fire station might be a better option.)

____

____

____

____

Transportation and Exchange Considerations (select all that apply)

[ ] Transportation of the child(ren) will be as follows (select only one):

[ ] The [ ] Mother [ ] Father shall typically provide all transportation for exchanges.

[ ] The parent ending their time-sharing shall provide transportation for the child(ren) (i.e. dropping the child(ren) off).

[ ] The parent beginning their time-sharing shall provide transportation for the child(ren) (i.e. picking the child(ren) up).

[ ] Both parents agree to have the child(ren) ready at the agreed upon time and with sufficient items to last the day, possibly including:

[ ] clothing for the day, [ ] including [ ] excluding pajamas
[ ] snow clothing (jacket, gloves/mittens, hat, snow boots)
[ ] medication, medical devices, glasses/contacts, retainers, hygiene products, etc.
[ ] electronic devices: computer, tablet, phone, watch.
[ ] school items including backpack, lunchbox and homework
[ ] extracurricular equipment and clothing for sports, music theater, etc.
[ ] other items as listed:

____

____

____

[ ] When the child(ren) turn ________ (age), the responsibility of ensuring they have all items needed for transferring to the other parent's home will be their responsibility.

[ ] If a parent is more than ________ (number of minutes) late, the parent with the child(ren) may consider the other parent a no-show and may deem the other parent's time cancelled.

[ ] In the event of a no-show by a parent for his/her parenting time, the time-sharing for that [ ] day [ ] full rotation [ ] other___________ will be deemed cancelled, unless agreed upon in writing.

[ ] If an essential item is forgotten, such as, but not limited to, medication, special equipment, uniforms, costumes, musical instruments, safety gear, school projects or other such shared items, the following will be the procedure:

____

____

____

____

____

[ ] Other agreements on transportation and exchanges of the child(ren):

____

____

____

____

____

[ ] The exchanges, if NOT done by the parents, will be done by:

____

____

[ ] A taxi or rideshare service specifically insured and equipped to transport minor children alone (and equipped with car seats) may be used.

____

____

Exchange or Transfer Transportation Costs

Routine transportation costs are often included in the state official child support calculations and/or the court order for child support. Discuss this with your attorney or legal professional to understand what is included in your area. However, non-routine and extraordinary transportation expenses, such as airfare, gas to travel long distances for exchanges, and any such transportation needed outside of the general and/or usual area can be handled as follows: (select only one)

[ ] The Mother shall pay ____% and the Father shall pay ___ % of the transportation costs.

[ ] Other:

____

____

____

____

____

____

F. FINANCIAL OBLIGATIONS FOR THE BENEFIT OF THE CHILD(REN)

Financial obligations post-divorce are handled differently according to your state and jurisdiction. Your jurisdiction may have a calculation method for child support payments between parents and what expenses that will cover, as well as specifics regarding parental rights and obligations. The court will have the final say over the amount(s) of child support between parents and what expenses are covered. In most states, this includes medical, medical insurance and K-12 education expenses, with some states requiring additional categories of expenses as well. Financial obligations related to childcare post-divorce should be discussed with your attorney or financial/legal professional to determine the allowable options in your case. Below are some examples of common expenses that are incurred as parents.

1. **Shared Extraordinary Expenses** (select all that apply)

[ ] Medical – The medical expenses for the child(ren) will be (select only one)
- [ ] shared in proportion to Mother's/Father's respective incomes
- [ ] paid by Mother _______ % Father _______ %
- [ ] Each parent will be billed by the service provider directly: Mother_ % Father _______ %

Medical expenses include all deductibles, expenses not covered by insurance, and extraordinary medical
expenses for the child(ren), including (select all that apply)

- [ ] co-pays and fees
- [ ] medical
- [ ] dental
- [ ] vision
- [ ] orthodontia
- [ ] counseling/therapy/psychiatric services
- [ ] prescriptions
- [ ] other as listed ____

____

____

[ ] School – The school expenses for the child(ren) will be (select only one)

- [ ] shared in proportion to Mother's/Father's respective incomes
- [ ] paid by Mother _______ % Father _______ %

School related costs and activities include (select all that apply)
- [ ] tuition/course and laboratory fees
- [ ] books or educational materials and fees
- [ ] school supplies
- [ ] exam and test prep classes, application fees
- [ ] college, trade school, or other secondary education application fees
- [ ] other as listed ____

____

____

[ ] Vocational or Trade School – The expenses for the child(ren) will be (select only one)

[ ] shared in proportion to Mother's/Father's respective incomes
[ ] paid by Mother _______ % Father _______ %

School related costs and activities include (select all that apply)
[ ] tuition/course and laboratory fees
[ ] books or educational materials and fees
[ ] school supplies
[ ] other as listed ____

____

____

[ ] Mobile phones and devices – The child(ren)'s phone expenses will be (select only one)
[ ] shared in proportion to Mother's/Father's respective incomes
[ ] paid by Mother _______ % Father _______ %

Where mobile phone and device costs include (select all that apply),
[ ] mobile phone/device purchases
[ ] mobile phone/device plan costs
[ ] insurance
[ ] repair
[ ] other as listed ____

____

____

[ ] Location tracking apps or software [ ] may [ ] may not, be put on the children's phones. All other surveillance, tracking, recording devices, hardware, software or apps are prohibited on or near the premises, property, or vehicles.

[ ] Extracurricular Activities – [ ] All activities [ ] Jointly approved activities expenses for the child(ren) will be (select only one)
[ ] shared in proportion to Mother's/Father's respective incomes
[ ] paid by Mother _______ % Father _______ %

[ ] paid by the parent requesting for them to participate

Where extracurricular activities include (select all that apply)

[ ] extracurricular sports/band equipment, uniforms
[ ] music lessons, instruments
[ ] camps and transportation
[ ] other as listed ____

____

____

[ ] Automotive Costs – The automotive expense for the child(ren) will be (select only one)

[ ] shared in proportion to Mother's/Father's respective incomes
[ ] paid by Mother _______ % Father _______ %
[ ] paid by Mother _______ % Father _______ % with the child(ren) responsible for the following list of related expenses:

____

____

Where automotive costs include (select all that apply)

[ ] vehicle purchase and tax not to exceed more than ________ (purchase amount)
[ ] insurance premiums
[ ] driver's education classes
[ ] driver's license costs
[ ] annual car registration, plates, and taxes
[ ] maintenance (such as brakes, tires, oil changes, fluid replacement)
[ ] gas, electric charging costs
[ ] vehicle repairs outside of warranty
[ ] other as listed ____

____

____

[ ] At age ______ the child(ren) will pay for their own expenses as follows:

[ ] expense ______________________________ at __________%
[ ] expense ______________________________ at __________%
[ ] expense ______________________________ at __________%
[ ] expense ______________________________ at __________%
[ ] expense ______________________________ at __________%

[ ] expense ______________________________ at __________%
[ ] expense ______________________________ at __________%
[ ] expense ______________________________ at __________%

[ ] Other agreements regarding expense sharing:

____

____

College and/or Trade School - Post-Secondary Education Costs

Legally, most parenting responsibilities end when your child emancipates (which is defined differently by state), unless there are special needs involved. That said, you still may want to create an agreement that includes some post-secondary education costs for college or trade school past the emancipation age. It is prudent to understand that any specific percentage for financial obligations could bind a parent beyond their financial means if factors and/or assumptions change (for example, a child ends up attending an expensive institution and/or one parent's income goes down substantially). Below are some options that can be discussed with your attorney or legal professional for inclusion in the parenting plan agreement.
(select all that apply)

[ ] Post-Secondary Savings – The parents agree to maintain the child(ren)'s 529 Plans or college savings accounts, with each parent contributing the following:

[ ] a minimum of _______% of their gross annual income to the child(ren)'s accounts per year

[ ] a minimum of $ _______ (amount) to the child(ren)'s account(s) per year.

[ ] Community college or Trade School
[ ] paid entirely by [ ] Mother [ ] Father [ ] Attending Child

[ ] loan provided by [ ] Mother [ ] Father [ ] Other
[ ] loan cosigned by [ ] Mother [ ] Father

[ ] shared in proportion to their respective incomes
[ ] shared with the following proportions: Mother ______ % Father _______ % attending Child _______ %

For the child(ren)'s related school costs including (select all that apply)

[ ] tuition and application fees
[ ] required books
[ ] room and board
[ ] travel
[ ] school supplies
[ ] lab, parking and other miscellaneous fees
[ ] other as listed____

____

____

[ ] 4-Year Undergrad College or University
[ ] paid entirely by [ ] Mother [ ] Father [ ] Attending Child
[ ] shared in proportion to their respective incomes
[ ] shared with the following proportions: Mother ______ % Father _______ % attending Child _______ %

For the child(ren)'s related school costs including (select all that apply)
[ ] tuition and application fees
[ ] required books
[ ] room and board
[ ] travel
[ ] school supplies
[ ] lab, parking and other miscellaneous fees
[ ] other as listed____

____

____

[ ] Graduate school (medica or law school, to obtain Masters or Ph.D.
[ ] paid entirely by [ ] Mother [ ] Father [ ] Attending Child
[ ] shared in proportion to their respective incomes
[ ] shared with the following proportions: Mother ______ % Father _______ % attending Child _______ %

For the child(ren)'s related school costs including (select all that apply)
[ ] tuition and application fees
[ ] required books
[ ] room and board
[ ] travel
[ ] school supplies
[ ] lab, parking and other miscellaneous fees
[ ] other as listed____

____

____

____

[ ] Other agreements between the parents for post-secondary education expenses:

____

____

____

____

____

2. Reporting and Payment Process

If the parents have agreed to share in some or all expenses, plan how the reporting and payment process will be handled. Always keep in mind the process that is established for the other parent will also apply to you. For example, if you agree that the expenses must be submitted within 30 days of incurring the expense, you will have to abide by the same agreed upon conditions.

[ ] The parents shall submit any requests for reimbursement to the other parent within ______ (time period) of incurring the expense by providing the other party with a copy of the bill/receipt and proof of payment.

[ ] The parents shall reimburse their share of the expense submitted by the other parent within _______ (time period) of receipt.

[ ] The expenses and reimbursements between co-parents will be handled as follows:

____

____

____

____

____

3. Expense Constraints and Protections

There is typically language in a parenting plan agreement describing the process for any expenses and reimbursements incurred by a parent in which the other parent has agreed, or will likely be court-ordered, to share in the expense. Agreeing in advance on how these are handled may be beneficial in some situations. (select all that apply)

[ ] Neither party shall be required to pay more than _______ (amount) for expenses per child, per year before the other party is required to reimburse.

[ ] A shared expense more than _______ (amount) must require the other parent's written approval prior to incurring the expense.

[ ] The parents agree any claims for reimbursements for the child(ren)'s expenses shall not be deducted from maintenance (alimony or spousal support) and child support payments.

[ ] The parents agree that if either parent does not make the payment of an agreed upon shared expense for the child(ren), the parent who is behind will handle all the fees associated with the pursuit of payment (including, but not limited to credit card interest, late fees, lawyer(s) fees, court fees, mediation fees, etc.)

4. Life and Disability Insurance Policy

While health insurance coverage for the child(ren) may be required in your state, this usually isn't the case for life or disability insurance. Since continued child support payment are important for the child(ren)'s welfare, having life insurance and/or disability insurance on the parent(s) may give added financial protections. This is most often included to cover the time, effort, supervision, maintenance/alimony and child-support between parents, but there may be other reasons to include it as well.

[ ] Mother [ ] Father [ ] Both parents will each own and pay for a life insurance policy with the other parent listed as the insured, naming themselves as the beneficiary to cover the total cost of maintenance and/or child support, for the following amounts:

[ ] Mother will own a policy on Father's life for _____________ (insurance amount) for_________ (number of years)

Policy Owner____
Named Beneficiary ____

[ ] Father will own a policy on Mother's life for ____________ (insurance amount) for_________ (number of years)
Policy Owner____
Named Beneficiary ____

[ ] Mother [ ] Father [ ] Both parents will maintain a disability insurance policy with the other parent listed as the insured, naming themselves as the beneficiary to cover the total costs of maintenance and/or child support, for the following amounts:

[ ] Mother will own a policy on Father for ____________ (insurance amount or percentage of income) for_________ (number of years)
Policy Owner____
Named Beneficiary ____

[ ] Father will own a policy on Mother for ____________ (insurance amount or percentage of income) for_________ (number of years)
Policy Owner____
Named Beneficiary ____

[ ] Other

____

____

____

[ ] After the youngest child reaches the age of majority/emancipation and all maintenance and/or child custody expense are paid and reimbursed, the owner will expedite the transfer of ownership (and the ability to change beneficiaries) to the other parent within _______ days of the other parent's request in writing.

5. Child Tax Benefits and Claiming the Child(ren)

In the United States, there are some recognizable tax benefits of listing children as dependent(s). It can make a difference on tax return payments or refunds. As there are often many factors involved, it is always best to consult a tax professional or accountant to determine the best options for your particular situation, keeping in mind that tax rules change. It is also recommended to keep track of medical, educational and other child(ren)-related expenses that may provide a tax benefit. Discuss these areas with a tax professional, certified divorce financial planner (CDFA) and/or your attorney to determine what would be beneficial to include in the parenting plan agreement. Below are some example options:

Child Tax Deductions or Benefits (select only one)

[ ] The available tax deductions or benefits for child(ren) will be claimed by
[ ] Mother [ ] Father [ ] Split equally between them.

[ ] Each parent will claim the children as agreed upon, unless the claim would not result in a tax benefit to one of them, in which case the other party is entitled to claim the child or children for tax purposes. The parent with the right to claim the child(ren) must notify the other parent as follows: (select only one)

[ ] within ______ (days/period of time) of learning they will not benefit from claiming the child(ren)

[ ] by ______________ (date) yearly

[ ] The available tax deductions or benefits for dependent child(ren) will be alternated every other year starting with [ ] Mother [ ] Father in ____________ (year).

[ ] The available tax deductions or benefits for the child(ren) will be split yearly as specified:

____

____

____

Other Child Tax Considerations (select all that apply)

[ ] A parent cannot claim the child as a dependent or for child tax credit or deduction if they are not up to date with all court-ordered child support and maintenance/alimony payments.

[ ] Any available tax deduction for the child(ren)'s medical expenses will be recognized by [ ] Mother [ ] Father [ ] Split _____% Mother _____% Father.

[ ] Any available tax deduction for the child(ren)'s educational expenses will be recognized by [ ] Mother [ ] Father [ ] Split _____% Mother _____% Father.

[ ] Other agreed upon tax situations:

____

____

____

____

____

____

G. OTHER CONSIDERATIONS

1. Child(ren)'s Surname / Last Name

While it is not always the case, often one of the parents may plan to change their name as part of, or after, the divorce. This can subsequently bring up questions on how to handle the children's surname following divorce. Some options include keeping the surname as is, creating a new hyphenated surname which incorporates both parents' surnames, using the last name of a new stepparent, or choosing an entirely different last name, for example, that of a grandparent.

The child(ren)'s age at the time of divorce may play a big role in the considerations for surname changes. Older children and teens may have strong feelings about what happens with their surname after the divorce. Below are some options to consider if a parent plans to change their own surname or it is an option for the child(ren) and clarification is needed.
(select all that apply)

[ ] The parents have agreed that the child(ren)'s surname after the divorce will be

____

[ ] The parents will discuss and agree on changes to the child(ren)'s surname in the future, if necessary. (After age 18, in many states, offspring are capable of petitioning the court themselves for a name change.)

[ ] Mother [ ] Father has the unilateral authority to change the child(ren)'s surname.

[ ] Any decision to change the surname will be made as follows: (select all that apply)

[ ] The child(ren) will keep the current surname ________________ until they become legal adults.

[ ] The child(ren) may choose their surname after they turn _________ (age).

[ ] Other agreements about the child(ren)'s surname:

____

____

____

____

2. Clothing, Equipment and Specialty Shared Items

While the belongings of the child(ren) may not seem like an important concern prior to divorce, it is a topic that can create significant contention between co-parents post-divorce. This is often a result of the parents viewing the items as their possessions and not belonging to the child(ren). Additionally, another common area that causes contention is when one parent ends up providing the child(ren) with the majority of their needed clothing and necessities, which ends up at the other parent's house or may get possibly lost. Here are some questions to consider:

- How will you deal with expensive clothing, car seats, or sports equipment?
- How do you plan to handle necessary items like a heavy winter coat, helmet, stroller, plack n' play, or sporting gear?
- What if expensive items get lost and do not come back from the other parent's residence?
- Who will replace lost or damaged items?
- What if one parent ends up paying for most of the expensive items?

Keeping situations like these in mind, it may be helpful to add some provisions around the child(ren)'s belongings in the parenting plan agreement. That said, it is still always best to consider the situation through the eyes of the child(ren) when it comes to the clothing and belongings, to make the exchange of the child(ren) as easy as possible and avoid resentment. (select all that apply)

[ ] Each parent will maintain sufficient clothing for the child(ren) at their house such that the child(ren) do not have to make the exchanges with additional clothing.

[ ] The child(ren) will be returned to the other parent with the clothing and belongings that they had when they arrived.

[ ] The following are specialty shared clothing items, such as heavy snow jackets, snow boots, insulated pants, protective clothing, helmets, eyewear, wetsuits, sports equipment, car seats, strollers, uniforms/costumes, etc., that will be shared and/or handled between houses as follows:

[ ] Item ____________________
Handled in the following manner________________________________
____

[ ] Item ____________________
Handled in the following manner________________________________
____

[ ] Item ____________________
Handled in the following manner________________________________
____

[ ] Item ____________________
Handled in the following manner________________________________
____

[ ] Item ____________________
Handled in the following manner________________________________
____

3. Significant Others and New Romantic Relationships

For some people, seeing the other parent introduce a new significant other to the children can raise concerns about safety, stability, and moral values. Statistically, on average, a new partner or stepparent may pose a slightly higher risk to children compared to the average biological parent. However, legally, you do not have the right to interview the new partner. You can request that the other parent refrain from introducing a new boyfriend or girlfriend too soon, to avoid exposing the children to a revolving door of adults in their lives. You can also request that the other parent get a basic background check on this new person, for their own sake.

While the other parent may not agree and the court is unlikely to enforce this request, it is still worth discussing: (select all that apply)

[ ] Both parents agree that if another person lives in the home while the children are there, they will inform the other parent of that person's full name and date of birth.

[ ] Both parents agree that a background check will be run on new romantic partners before they are introduced the children, and that no one will be introduced if there is any criminal arrest, conviction, or incarceration.

[ ] Both parents agree that if a background check reveals any criminal arrest, conviction, or incarceration in the new romantic partner, more parenting time will temporarily be given to the other parent.

[ ] The parents agree that neither party will introduce a new significant other to the child(ren) until that relationship has existed for _____________ (timeframe).

[ ] The parents agree that they will not have a non-married romantic partner sleep over in the same house when the children are there.

[ ] The parents agree the child(ren) will have separate sleeping quarters from the adults. (This is a legal requirement in most states.)

[ ] The significant other [ ] may [ ] may not care for the child(ren) in the parent's absence.

[ ] The significant other [ ] may [ ] may not discipline the child(ren) in the parent's absence.

[ ] The significant other will be referred to as ________________________________

[ ] The parents agree that <u>only</u> the child(ren)'s legal parents will be referred to or addressed as Mom or Dad post-divorce:

[ ] Mother with be referred or addressed as "Mom or Mother"
[ ] Father will be referred or addressed as "Dad or Father."
[ ] Other

____

____

____

[ ] For purposes of emergency contact information for the child(ren) (for example, school, medical, etc.), the parents will always be listed prior to any other significant other, with the legal relationship designated after each name: "Mother," "friend," "neighbor," "stepparent" etc.

[ ] The new partner will participate in decisions regarding the child(ren) as follows:

____

____

____

____

[ ] Other agreements regarding the introduction of a new significant other:

____

____

____

____

____

4. Dual Citizenship

While not extremely common, sometimes one or both parents would like the child(ren) to obtain dual citizenship with another country. This most commonly occurs when one or both parents are from different countries, and therefore, may be citizens of another country or have dual citizenship themselves. (select only one)

[ ] The parents agree that the child(ren) will <u>not</u> become citizens of any other country until they are of adult age and decide this for themselves.

[ ] The parents agree when the child(ren) are ______ (age), they will present the child(ren) the opportunity to become dual citizens with ____________ ____ (country/list of countries). However, ultimately it will be the child(ren)'s decision. This application process will be handled by [ ] Mother [ ] Father
It will be paid for by [ ] Mother [ ] Father

[ ] The parents agree that the child(ren) will become dual citizens with ______________ (country), regardless of the age of the child(ren). This application process will be handled by [ ] Mother [ ] Father.

[ ] The child(ren) will have dual citizenship, but only one passport for the following country: _______________

[ ] Other

____

____

____

____

____

____

5. Pets / Animals

Pets are a very special part of many families and sometimes get overlooked in the divorce process. There are several ways to cover the arrangement of the pet(s), should you feel this would be beneficial to include. For example, having the pet(s) go with the child(ren) can certainly be an option if acceptable to both parents. However, sometime only one parent is attached to the pet(s), in which case the pet(s) future may be easier to determine. That said, if the pet was introduced into the home during the marriage, parents may want to negotiate who pays expenses such as food, litter, medication, grooming, kenneling, routine/emergency veterinarian care, boarding during vacations, toys, etc. : (select all that apply)

[ ] Pet _____________________ (pet's name) will:
  [ ] follow the child(ren)'s schedule
  [ ] stay with [ ] Mother [ ] Father
  [ ] other

[ ] Pet _____________________ (pet's name) will:
  [ ] follow the child(ren)'s schedule
  [ ] stay with [ ] Mother [ ] Father
  [ ] other

[ ] Pet _____________________ (pet's name) will:
  [ ] follow the child(ren)'s schedule
  [ ] stay with [ ] Mother [ ] Father
  [ ] other

[ ] Pet _____________________ (pet's name) will:
  [ ] follow the child(ren)'s schedule

[ ] stay with [ ] Mother [ ] Father
[ ] other

[ ] Each party will be responsible for day-to-day expenses for the pet(s)/animals while that party has physical custody. The day-to-day expenses include, but are not limited to:

[ ] food
[ ] toys
[ ] accessories
[ ] walking expenses
[ ] daycare
[ ] grooming
[ ] boarding
[ ] other as specified below:

____
____
____
____

[ ] The parties will split expenses for veterinary visits, medications, and other agreed upon medical expenses for the pet(s) as follows:

[ ] Mother ______% Father ______%

[ ] Other arrangement: ______________________________
____
____

[ ] The parties agree to divide the following pet expense as follows:

Expense Item ____________________ Mother ______% Father______%
Expense Item ____________________ Mother ______% Father ______%
Expense Item ____________________ Mother ______% Father ______%
Expense Item ____________________ Mother ______% Father ______%
Expense Item ____________________ Mother ______% Father ______%
Expense Item ____________________ Mother ______% Father ______%
Expense Item ____________________ Mother ______% Father ______%
Expense Item ____________________ Mother ______% Father ______%

6. Religious Considerations

Sometimes the topic of religious education and traditions for the child becomes an area of disagreement after divorce even though the couple agreed while married. You can offer a compromise, or allow the children to choose for themselves at a certain age. (select all that apply)

[ ] The parents agree to continue to raise the child(ren) with the spiritual beliefs taught in the household prior to the divorce.

[ ] The parents agree that the child(ren)'s religious upbringing/training will be as follows: (select all that apply)

[ ] The child(ren) will be raised as ______________________________________

[ ] The child(ren) will be taught by [ ] Mother [ ] Father [ ] Both parents the religious beliefs as follows:

____

____

____

____

____

____

____

[ ] The child(ren) may choose their religious affiliation and the house of worship they wish to attend.

____

____

[ ] The parents agree that at age _____ the child(ren) can decide on their own their religious affiliation and their attendance at church services or events.

[ ] The child(ren) may choose their religious training and affiliation

[ ] Regardless of age or what religion they are choosing
[ ] At ________ (age)

[ ] Other agreements related to the child(ren)'s religious beliefs:

____

____

____

____

____

7. Alternative Dispute Resolution and Noncompliance

Most likely the state or jurisdiction you are divorcing in will have a court-mandated form that provides specific language and structure around managing disputes in the court post-divorce. Check with your attorney or a legal professional for specifics in your jurisdiction. The first checkbox in the following list gives an example with common language for a standard alternative dispute resolution process. However, there may be additional situations that you foresee where you would like to have other conflict resolution steps in place prior to a court-ordered dispute management process. One common situation is when a co-parent does not fully comply with the Parenting Plan Agreement. In this case, it can be very helpful to have a statement about who will pay the court fees in the event of non-compliance, giving the non-compliant parent a greater incentive to follow the agreement. Below are some options to consider: (select all that apply)

[ ] If any disputes arise with regard to the parenting plan, the parents agree to schedule and actively participate in mediation. The mediator shall be jointly chosen, and if the parents cannot agree, the mediator will be appointed by the court.

[ ] If disagreements arise that are not resolved, the parents agree to participate with third party assistance as follows in an effort to resolve the conflict. (select all that apply)

[ ] counseling/therapy
[ ] meeting with attorney(s)
[ ] mediation
[ ] arbitration
[ ] family member(s) as listed ______________________________
[ ] other ____

____

[ ] If unresolved conflict continues regarding the parenting plan agreement, the parents agree to the following: (select all that apply)

[ ] Mother has the authority to make the final decision regarding (specify)

____

____

[ ] Father has the authority to make the final decision regarding (specify)

____

____

[ ] The following individual/authority will make the final decision

____

[ ] No changes will be made unless both parents agree. If they cannot find a solution, common ground or a compromise, they will follow the court's guidelines for dispute resolution with the fees being paid by
[ ] Mother [ ] Father.

[ ] The parents agree that if either parent is non-compliant and/or in violation of the parenting agreement, the party that is in violation will pay all the fees associated with the pursuit of compliance (i.e. attorney(s) fees, court fees, arbitration fees, etc.)

[ ] Other agreements for alternative dispute resolution and non-compliance:

____

____

____

____

8. Review and Modifications

Being forward thinking when designing the initial parenting plan agreement can help minimize the changes that would otherwise need to be made to the agreement over time. As child(ren) go from totally dependent to nearly independent, their needs will change, and the parenting plan will need to adjust. It is always best for the child(ren) when the parents can work together collaboratively to review and modify the parenting plan agreement. That said, that may not always be possible given the dynamics between the parents and if there is a high-conflict co-parent involved.

Below are some ideas to consider if having explicit modification provisions would prove beneficial for you in your situation. (select all that apply)

[ ] We will review the Parenting Plan as follows:

[ ] ________________________ (specify frequency)
[ ] at graduation from elementary, middle, and high school
[ ] when problems arise

[ ] Reviews will be handled by

[ ] phone call
[ ] in person
[ ] email.

[ ] Reviews will be handled with additional assistance through

[ ] counseling
[ ] mediation
[ ] arbitration
[ ] family member(s) or trusted friend(s) as listed:
____
____
____
____

[ ] other
____
____

[ ] The parents agree that the child(ren) may share their preferences and concerns in the discussions when they are over the age of ______.

[ ] The parents agree that the child(ren) may have a say in the decisions.

[ ] If a substantive modification is needed in the parenting plan agreement that is agreed by both parents, [ ] Mother [ ] Father [ ] the parent that is initiating the change, will prepare (or ensure that someone else prepares, such as an attorney) a summary of the agreement modifications so that a court order may be obtained incorporating the changes.

[ ] Each parent will be responsible to review the agreement prior to its submission to the court and/or seek independent advice at their own cost on the

modifications to the agreement.

[ ] The costs incurred for modifications to the parenting plan agreement will be handled as follows: (select one)

[ ] The costs will be paid by [ ] Mother [ ] Father.

[ ] The costs will be split by individual percentages as follows:
[ ] Mother with _______% [ ] Father with _______ %.

[ ] The costs will be split according to the income split as decided by the court.

[ ] Other (specify)

____

____

[ ] Other agreements for review and modifications of the parenting plan:

____

____

____

____

9. Other Concerns or Issues

____

____

____

____

____

____

____

____

____

____

10. Explanation of Special Circumstances

The following space is provided to detail any special circumstances as well as explanations (such as legal issues, medical needs, special accommodations, therapy, schooling, etc.) Explain the circumstances as much as possible, including details such as experts who have been consulted, court or law enforcement involvement, medical issues and/or any detailed accommodations that should be considered for the child(ren). This can be presented to your attorney or divorce professional to help them understand the specific needs of your child(ren).

4

JOINT CUSTODY CONSIDERATIONS

Children's needs and wishes change as they get older.
Create a plan that can adapt.

JOINT CUSTODY CONSIDERATIONS – SECTION 4

Time-sharing, also commonly known as custody and parenting time, is the physical time that the child(ren) spends with each parent during separation or divorce. It asks: "What is the best for the child(ren); and how many days per year will the child(ren) live with each parent?" In general, it is best for the child(ren) to have as much stability and safety as possible to reduce any big changes, conflict, or stress from the divorce. If the child(ren) was doing well prior to the divorce, it is often good to keep things the way they were, without switching schools, losing friendships and moving away from nurturing family members. Some parents have occupations that make it difficult, if not impossible, to care for the children half of the time. Additionally, the time spent with each parent may impact child-support payments which are commonly calculated using the percentage of time spent with each parent. The child(ren) will benefit greatly if parents can cooperate in creating a time-sharing agreement focused on **the child(ren)'s needs** and not which parent receives more time or how it may impact the child-support payments.

A note about abuse: *If there is spousal or child abuse in the home, it may be prudent to put some distance between yourself and the other parent, including moving closer to your family. That's the exception to the "no big changes" rule. Moving may be best to do before you file for divorce. Ask your attorney about the legal aspects.*

When designing a time-sharing plan, there are many factors to consider, and every family is different. However, it is of the utmost importance to consider the schedule through the eyes of your child(ren), as they will be the ones living the arrangement. Predictability, stability and cooperation between the parents are important to the child(ren)'s wellbeing in the long run.

Below are some of the most common questions and considerations that arise when developing a time-sharing plan:

Age and developmental stage: The age, as well as their subsequent developmental stage, may impact the frequency and length of time physically spent with each parent. For babies and children under three, it is important to consider what percentage of time each parent is interested in and/or capable of managing. Likewise, for teens it is important to consider if a rigid schedule may only cause greater issues as they grow older and navigate teen years, striving for a greater voice and influence in their lives. That said, be sure to check with your attorney or legal professional if there is an age at which children are allowed to have a say in the custody arrangement, or not, in your area.

What is the age and developmental stage of the child(ren)?

Parental Involvement: While this can be a tricky subject to navigate, it is important to try and take an objective view of the current, pre-separation/divorce level of involvement of each parent with the child(ren). For example, if one parent travels most of the time and then has hobbies that fill his/her time on the weekend, they may not have a strong, active relationship with the child(ren) at the time of the divorce. This is not to say that it won't improve, but it may be worthwhile to consider if that parent may not be immediately ready, emotionally or otherwise, to become a 50/50 time-sharing co-parent. Likewise, the child(ren) may not be ready, causing difficulties and potentially emotional issues for them. In cases like this, a "step-up" approach may benefit all parties where the time-sharing split starts out closer to the current level of parental involvement prior to divorce and then increases overtime, for example, the time-sharing could start at 70/30 and over a defined period of time, become 50/50.

Describe the level of involvement of each parent with the child(ren). What percentage of time a day, a week, do each parent actively spend with the child(ren)?

Gender: The gender of the child(ren) may influence scheduling needs and should be taken into consideration. To ease exchanges, ensure that duplicate items are available at each parent's home, such as feminine products and other essentials, that may help the child(ren) feel comfortable at both homes.

What is the gender of the child(ren)? How may this impact the time-sharing needs of the child(ren)?

Temperament: The needs of the child(ren) may inform the frequency of contact with each parent as well as the ability to tolerate frequent, or infrequent, exchanges.

Explain any needs or temperament issues that may affect the child's ability to have frequent transfers from home to home.

Geographical Location: The geographical proximity of the parents' homes should be considered when designing a plan. Travel time between houses, as well as to/from school or other common activities, can have a substantial impact on your child(ren) and their adaptability to the time-sharing arrangement.

What is the geographical location of the parents' homes? Is there any possibility that the locations may change over the period that the time-sharing agreement will be in place? If so, how would that be handled? Should definition of responsibility for transportation costs be included in the parenting plan?

Special Needs or Neurodiversity: Any special needs of the child(ren) should be carefully evaluated and discussed with your attorney when designing the time-sharing schedule. It is important to consider whether both parents are able to meet the needs and if they have the available resources for support if needed.

What are the special needs of the child(ren)? What accommodations are currently in place or may need to be in place in the future?

____
____
____
____
____
____
____

Same vs. Differing Schedules: When creating a schedule for multiple children impacted by the divorce, it is important to remember that they do not have to be on the exact same schedule. Some parents like to create some one-on-one time in the schedule for separate children. Contrarily, depending on their closeness and/or personalities, having children on the same schedule may help create a feeling of greater security for the child(ren).

Should the same schedule be used for all of your children? What would be the benefits, and downsides, to having the children on different schedules? On the same schedule?

____
____
____
____
____
____
____
____

Parent Work Schedules: Differing work schedules may influence the time-scheduling plan due to the availability of the parent(s) to pick up the child(ren) from school or other activities.

Explain the current work schedules of each parent. Are there any work schedule constraints or circumstances that need to be accounted for in the time-sharing agreement? Are any changes to work schedules expected post-divorce?

Needs of Adolescents: A consideration commonly overlooked during the process of creating a time-sharing schedule is the needs of the child(ren) as they grow older. For example, a time-sharing arrangement for your toddler will likely need to be adjusted as they grow into teenagers. Ensuring flexibility and adaptability for changes as your child(ren) age is helpful for the long-term success of a time-sharing plan. Additionally, building a parenting plan and time-sharing agreement that incorporates the child(ren)'s maturity and independence can save both time and money by minimizing the modifications needed as well as the stress on the child(ren).

How do you think the child(ren) will feel about time-sharing schedules as they grow older? Explain what you expect will be your child(ren)'s current biggest challenge – and possible future challenges with a time-schedule arrangement.

Input from the Child(ren): Knowing your children's personalities, how much input do you expect your child(ren) to want in deciding on a time-sharing schedule? Some judges consider child(ren)'s wishes about time-sharing; others do not. It may be best to find out in advance which view your courts and/or judge hold.

What do you feel is the "right" amount of input, if any, for your child(ren) to have in the time-sharing considerations at their current age? And explain why you feel this way. Do you feel the amount of input they have should change as they age? And, if so, explain why.

____

____

____

____

____

____

____

____

5

TIME-SHARING SCHEDULES & SAMPLE CALENDARS

Sample calendars for 50/50, 60/40, 70/30, and 80/20 time sharing.

Time-Sharing Scheduling and Sample Calendars – SECTION 5

Most courts and jurisdictions typically will favor an equal division of time between parents (i.e., approximately a 50/50 split). In fact, many states have adopted statutes stating equal parenting time as the default in divorce proceedings, unless a demonstrable need for a different time allocation can be shown. Therefore, an agreement between parents outside of court may provide the best opportunity to tailor the division of time to best suit the needs of the child(ren) as well as the parents (i.e. where a 50/50 arrangement is not optimal for the child(ren) or a particular parent).

Once a time-sharing schedule has been determined, all family members, especially the child(ren), should have a copy of the schedule that is accessible, including dates and times. A color-coded calendar posted in a common household space, such as on the refrigerator or near the door or an online calendar that clearly shows the schedule may be helpful. Having the schedule easily available can help to alleviate anxiety and help the child(ren) prepare both emotionally and physically for the transfer between houses.

Below are some common time-sharing percentages and corresponding example time-sharing calendars.

- **50/50** schedules are often the default of many courts. They are designed so that the child(ren) spend an equal number of days with each parent. Some common 50/50 schedules include ***Alternating Weeks*** or the ***3-4-4-3 day*** and ***5-2-2-5 day rotation*** schedules.

- A **60/40** arrangement is a parenting time division in which one parent cares for the child(ren) 60% of the time, with the other parent providing 40% of physical custody. This time-sharing schedule still gives significant time for each parent with the child(ren). Some common 60/40 schedules include the ***4-3 day rotation*** and the ***Every Extended Weekend*** schedule, where one parent has the child(ren) Monday through Friday and the other parent has the weekends.

- A **70/30** schedule is one which allows a child(ren) to have more of a "home base" with one parent but still spend time with the other parent. Some common 70/30 schedules include the ***5-2 day rotation*** and ***Every 3rd Week*** schedule, where one parent takes the first, second and last week of every month and the other parent has the third week.

- An **80/20** schedule is where the child(ren) lives primarily with one parent, at 80% of the time, spending considerably less time in the care of the other parent at 20% of the time. A common schedule for this arrangement is the ***Alternating Weekends*** schedule with the children spending every other weekend with the non-primary physical custody parent.

What if the other parent has engaged in illegal behavior?

Time-Sharing with a Phased or Stepped-up Approach

Some courts require the child(ren) to have time with both parents, regardless of criminal behavior or substance addition issues. If this is the situation in your jurisdiction, one idea is to propose a ***stepped-up*** parenting plan. Your attorney or legal professional may want to modify this to better suit your specific case. See one woman's story below.

In the table below, "Parent A" has a history of substance abuse, violence, criminal behavior, and/or anger issues while "Parent B" has primary custody.

Phase	Parent A's actions	Parenting time
Phase 1	Parent A is not in any weekly court-approved treatment program or has no evidence to verify attendance and progress. Parent A has not been sober for at least 30 days.	Monitored visitation. 1-3 hours per week, paid for by Parent A.
Phase 2	Parent A has been enrolled in a weekly court-approved treatment program at least 90 days and currently has evidence to prove regular attendance, sobriety, and significant progress. That is signed by program director.	70/30 Parenting time (70% to Parent B; 30% to Parent A)
Phase 3	Parent A has successfully completed and graduated from a court-approved program and is currently sober and attending recommended follow-ups and weekly programs, such as Alcoholics Anonymous. This should be signed by a program director and monthly accountability signed by their sponsor. No law enforcement investigations or arrests.	60/40 Parenting time
Phase 4	Parent A has successfully completed and graduated from a court-approved program, attends weekly program such as Alcoholics Anonymous, and has been sober one year or more. Weekly attendance and accountability signed by sponsor. No law enforcement investigations or arrests.	50/50 Parenting time

If there is a DUI or DV incident or arrest or loss of sobriety, or if they drop out of the program, fail to get signatures from directors or sponsors, or are considered a "treatment failure," parenting time reverts to Phase 1.

One woman tells her story:

"I was married to an alcoholic who also used methamphetamines and abused me. Some judges might automatically give the fit stable parent sole custody, but not mine. I had to show the court some level of cooperation to restore their father to their life if he was attempting to improve himself. At the same time, I had to keep the kids and myself safe.

My attorney wanted me to put together a simple parenting plan with no changes for holidays. He told me I could give my ex-husband extra time if he seemed healthy and safe enough.

My attorney added a stepped-up plan for visitation.

My ex-husband kept signing up for new rehabilitation programs trying to delay court proceedings. He was still in the middle of one when it was time to finalize our custody plan. My attorney and I suspected my ex was enrolling in rehab classes to present well in court and try to win me back. I told my attorney I was certain he'd drop out of the program once he saw it wasn't going to work.

Since he was still in rehab and had openly confessed his major meth and alcohol use, Phase 1 meant he was only seeing the children for two hours on the weekends, and it was supervised.

Phase 2 required him to be in a program and sober for 90 days. Phase 3 could only happen if my ex-husband completed the rehab program and provided proof of successful completion.

My ex dropped out of the church-based recovery program but still went to church. I let him move into Phase 2. But then he went off the deep end with drugs and alcohol. I was able to flex the parenting plan and reverted to Phase 1 until he provided proof of program completion signed by the program director.

It was a bit of drama and a couple months before he saw the kids at all, but they were able to be home safe with me instead of getting dragged into the mess he had created.

When my ex started making noise about his "rights," the mediator told him that his wishes didn't get included in the plan because he hadn't asked for them. She reminded him that he had agreed to and had signed the custody plan. He was offended that it wasn't going his way and stormed out of mediation instead of advocating for an official change in wording.

I think my attorney's insight really worked in my kids' favor here."

Time-Sharing Schedule and Calendar Examples

The following section provides some visual example schedules of various time-sharing schedule plans. When designing a time-sharing schedule, it is important to consider at what time the exchange will take place. For example, if the child(ren) is in school on an exchange day, setting a time after school at pick-up time may be a good approach. Alternatively, you may feel a time before school is better for your child(ren). On weekends, a different time may be preferred.

Alternating Weeks is a common 50/50 schedule where both parents alternate weeks with the child(ren). It may not be the best schedule for babies or very young children who have difficulty being away from either parent for extended periods of time, or even older child(ren) with a greater established attachment to one parent, as this schedule results in 7 full nights away from each parent for every rotation.

Examples of 50/50 Time-Sharing Schedules

Alternating Weeks (50/50)

Sunday	Monday	Tuesday	Wednesday	Thursday	Friday	Saturday
	1	2	3	4	5 3:00	6
7	8	9	10	11	12 3:00	13
14	15	16	17	18	19 3:00	20
21	22	23	24	25	26 3:00	27
28	29	30	31			

50% ______________________________(Parent A) 50% ______________________________(Parent B)

The 3-4-4-3 Plan (also known as the 4-3-3-4 Plan) is also a 50/50 schedule but does not create the long periods away from each parent. However it increases the movement of the child(ren), their homework, and belongings. This version of the 3-4-4-3 plan below results in one parent having all weekends, and the other parent having weekdays.

3-4-4-3 Plan (50/50)

Sunday	Monday	Tuesday	Wednesday	Thursday	Friday	Saturday
	1	2	3 3:00 pm	4	5	6
7 12:00 pm	8	9	10	11 3:00 pm	12	13
14 12:00 pm	15	16	17 3:00 pm	18	19	20
21 12:00 pm	22	23	24	25 3:00 pm	26	27
28 12:00 pm	29	30	31 3:00 pm			

50% ________________________________(Parent A) 50% ________________________________(Parent B)

The 2-2-5-5 Plan (also known as the 5-2-2-5) is another 50/50 time-sharing plan which is similar to the 3-4-4-3 plan above, but increases the longer period from 4 to 5 days and decreases the shorter period from 3 to 2 days. Having the longer period in one place may be preferred, but keep in mind that the shorter 2-day rotations can feel like a lot of activity for some child(ren). That said, this is a popular schedule with courts trying to come up with a 50/50 plan where each parent gets a full alternating weekend.

2-2-5-5 Plan (50/50)

Sunday	Monday	Tuesday	Wednesday	Thursday	Friday	Saturday
	1 3:00 pm	2	3 3:00 pm	4	5 3:00 pm	6
7	8	9	10 3:00 pm	11	12	13
14	15 3:00 pm	16	17 3:00 pm	18	19 3:00 pm	20
21	22	23	24 3:00 pm	25	26	27
28	29 3:00 pm	30	31 3:00 pm			

50% ________________________(Parent A) 50% ________________________(Parent B)

The 2-2-3 Plan is a 50/50 time-sharing plan, which appears at first glance that it may not be an equal parenting time split. However, the third day rotation is alternated between the parents, creating a 50/50 time-sharing split. In this case, the parents each have a 2-day rotation followed by a 3-day rotation, which ends up alternating between them. This schedule eliminates any period longer than 3 nights at one house, which can feel like a lot of change for the child(ren). Likewise, there are no designated days always spent with one parent, which can also get confusing and less stabilizing for the child(ren). On the positive side, it does eliminate longer periods away from either parent while still providing each parent to have full, alternating weekends with the child(ren).

2-2-3 Plan (50/50)

Sunday	Monday	Tuesday	Wednesday	Thursday	Friday	Saturday
	1 3:00 pm	2	3 3:00 pm	4	5 3:00 pm	6
7	8 3:00 pm	9	10 3:00 pm	11	12 3:00 pm	13
14	15 3:00 pm	16	17 3:00 pm	18	19 3:00 pm	20
21	22 3:00 pm	23	24 3:00 pm	25	26 3:00 pm	27
28	29 3:00 pm	30	31 3:00 pm			

50% ______________________________(Parent A) 50% ______________________________(Parent B)

Examples of 60/40 Time-Sharing Schedules

The 4-3 Plan is similar to the 3-4-4-3 plan, but creates a 60/40 time distribution instead by allotting 4 days with one parent and 3 with the other on a rotating basis. This plan does allow for certain days to be designated with one particular parent (for example, a child will understand they are always at Mom's house on Sunday, Monday, Tuesday nights and with Dad every Wednesday, Thursday and Friday nights) and creates a schedule where the child(ren) are not away from either parent for extended periods of time. However, it does not provide both parents with equal weekend time with the child(ren).

4-3 Plan (60/40)

Sunday	Monday	Tuesday	Wednesday	Thursday	Friday	Saturday
	1	2	3 3:00 pm	4	5	6 5:00 pm
7	8	9	10 3:00 pm	11	12	13 5:00 pm
14	15	16	17 3:00 pm	18	19	20 5:00 pm
21	22	23	24 3:00 pm	25	26	27 5:00 pm
28	29	30	31 3:00 pm			

40% ______________________________(Parent A) 60% ______________________________(Parent B)

The 5-4-3-2 Plan is another variation on the previous schedule as one parent gets one more day with each rotation than the other parent. This plan avoids the child(ren) from being away from any parent for longer than 5 days, which may be beneficial for some children, while also providing each parent with full weekends with the child(ren). That said, the trade-off is that the 3-day and 2-day rotations may feel like a lot of transitioning for the child(ren). One positive aspect of this plan is its ability to migrate into a plan where the child(ren) have a homebase with one parent – turning into a 70/30 arrangement if the 2-day rotation is eliminated (see the *10-4 Plan)*. Likewise, if you have two children on different plans, one needing a 70/30 time-sharing split and the other with a 60/40 time-sharing split, this plan can work well to keep the child(ren) on relatively similar schedules.

5-4-3-2 (60/40)

Sunday	Monday	Tuesday	Wednesday	Thursday	Friday	Saturday
	1	2	3 3:00	4	5	6
7 7:00	8	9	10 3:00	11	12 3:00	13
14	15	16	17 3:00	18	19	20
21 7:00	22	23	24 3:00	25	26 3:00	27
28	29	30	31 3:00			

60% ______________________________(Parent A) 40% ______________________________(Parent B)

Examples of 70/30 Time-Sharing Schedules

Every 3rd Week is a 70/30 time-sharing schedule. This provides the child(ren) with a long period of time with one parent as a "home base" and reduces the constant back and forth while also providing one full weekend and 7 overnights with the other parent.

Every 3rd Week - (70/30)

Sunday	Monday	Tuesday	Wednesday	Thursday	Friday	Saturday
	1	2	3	4	5	6
7	8	9	10	11	12 3:00	13
14	15	16	17	18	19 3:00	20
21	22	23	24	25	26	27
28	29	30	31			

70% ______________________________(Parent A) 30% ______________________________(Parent B)

The **Every Weekend** schedule results in a 70/30 time-sharing split if the exchanges occur on Friday and Sunday. The schedule can work well for parents needing a 70/30 split, for example where one parent may work the weekend or there is a parent who travels a lot. However, it does not provide the opportunity for the child(ren) to have weekend time with both parents.

Every Weekend - (70/30)

Sunday	Monday	Tuesday	Wednesday	Thursday	Friday	Saturday
	1	2	3	4	5 3:00	6
7 5:00	8	9	10	11	12 3:00	13
14 5:00	15	16	17	18	19 3:00	20
21 5:00	22	23	24	25	26 3:00	27
28 5:00	29	30	31			

70% ____________________________(Parent A) 30% ____________________________(Parent B)

The **10-4** schedule is a 70/30 time-sharing split where the child(ren) stays with one parent for 10 nights before transitioning for 4 nights to the other parent. This plan works when one parent travels frequently, as they have solid blocks of time in which they know they can travel without conflicting with their parenting time. Likewise, it provides the child(ren) with a solid amount of time between exchanges, providing more stability. While this schedule may not suit smaller children who are sometimes uncomfortable being away from one parent for too long, it may be a good solution for older child(ren) and teens. Likewise, this plan coordinates well with the 5-4-3-2 (60/40) plan if you need two different plans for your children and/or if you feel it may benefit to start with one plan and move to the other one over time (also referred to as a "step-up" or "step-down" plan). For example, if the child(ren) is not as accustomed to being alone with one parent, and/or the parent is unable to provide care for the child(ren) with a 60/40 time-split, the co-parents could start with this plan and move towards the 5-4-3-2 plan when the time is right for the child(ren) or parents.

10-4 (70/30)

Sunday	Monday	Tuesday	Wednesday	Thursday	Friday	Saturday
	1	2	3 3:00	4	5	6
7 7:00	8	9	10	11	12	13
14	15	16	17 3:00	18	19	20
21 7:00	22	23	24	25	26	27
28	29	30	31 3:00			

60% ______________________(Parent A) 40% ______________________(Parent B)

Examples of 80/20 Time-Sharing Schedules

The **Alternating Weekend** schedule is a popular choice for co-parents needing an 80/20 time-sharing split. This schedule may work well for a situation in which one of the parent travels often or where it is beneficial for the child(ren) to live primarily with one parent. It creates a lot of stability for the child(ren) due to the lack of back and forth while still providing quality weekend time with both parents.

Alternating Weekends - (80/20)

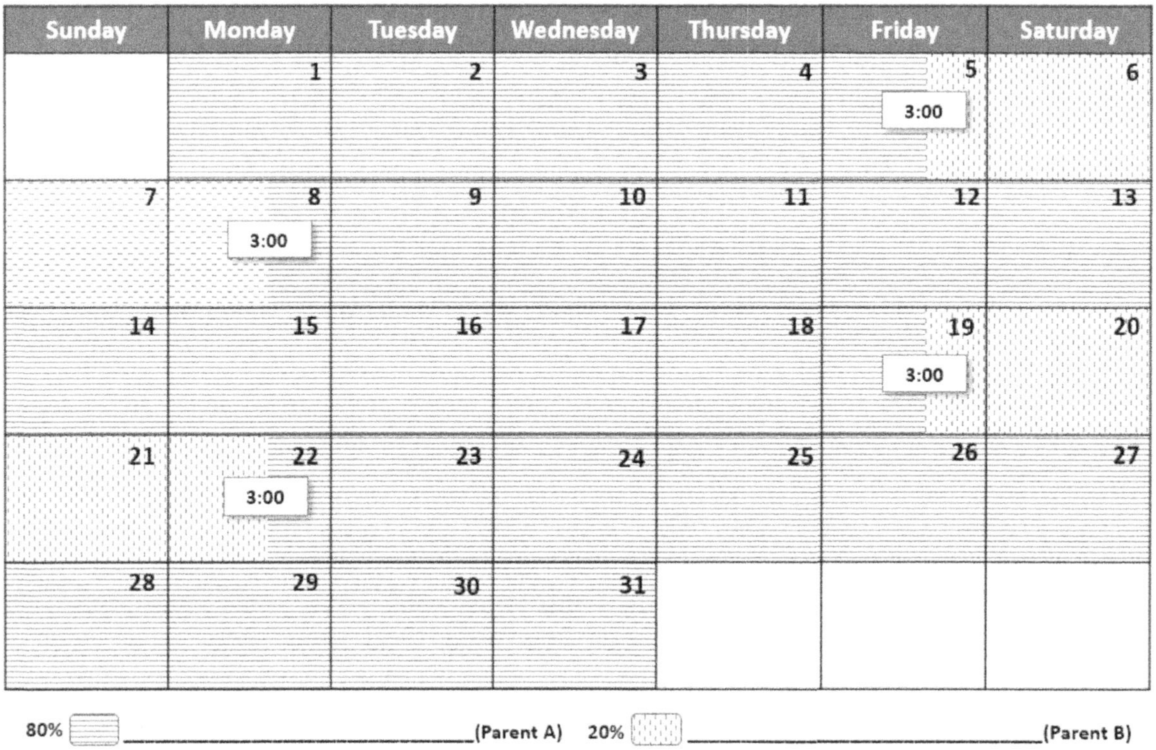

6

PLAN A, B, AND C EXERCISE

PLAN A, B, AND C EXERCISE – SECTION 6

What if you and the other parent cannot come to an agreement and the court will not make a decision on a particular issue? Given that you and your co-parent may not agree on all components of the parenting plan, the Plan A, B, and C Exercise outlined below can be a useful tool to assist in journaling what areas you are willing to negotiate in order to get agreement in the areas that you really want for your child(ren). Consider working with your attorney, a mediator, or even a shared counselor to help facilitate the conversation, but it is recommended that you do not share the answers you have filled into your workbook to the other parent or child custody evaluator without your attorney or legal professional's approval.

Plan A: The Ideal Arrangement for the Child(ren)

Top 10 issues I feel are in the best interest of the child(ren)

1.____
2.____
3.____
4.____
5.____
6.____
7.____
8.____
9.____
10._______________________________________

Put yourself in your co-parent's shoes and list out the top 5 items that you believe he/she would want included in the parenting plan agreement:

1.____
2.____
3.____
4.____
5.____

Plan B: An Acceptable Compromise

Sometimes you and your co-parent will need to negotiate and compromise to get an agreement in writing. Be prepared to trade and give-and-take if this is the case.

I can compromise on these issues for the child(ren):

I am less willing to compromise on these issues for the child(ren):

Plan C: A Further Compromise if Required by the Court

If required, I can compromise on these issues for the child(ren):

I am less willing to compromise on these issues for the child(ren):

NOTES

Made in the USA
Monee, IL
05 November 2026

67845309R20072